OCT 1 6 2017

China

China

BY NEL YOMTOV

Enchantment of the World™
Second Series

CHILDREN'S PRESS®

An Imprint of Scholastic Inc.

Frontispiece: **Fisher in Guangxi Province**

Consultant: Zhiqun Zhu, PhD, Associate Professor of Political Science and International Relations, Inaugural Director of the China Institute, Bucknell University, Lewisburg, PA
Please note: All statistics are as up-to-date as possible at the time of publication.

Book production by The Design Lab

Library of Congress Cataloging-in-Publication Data
Names: Yomtov, Nelson, author.
Title: China / by Nel Yomtov.
Description: New York : Children's Press, an imprint of Scholastic Inc., [2017] | Series:
    Enchantment of the world | Includes bibliographical references and index.
Identifiers: LCCN 2016056323 | ISBN 9780531235713 (library binding : alk. paper)
Subjects: LCSH: China—Juvenile literature.
Classification: LCC DS706 .Y56 2017 | DDC 951—dc23
LC record available at https://lccn.loc.gov/2016056323

All rights reserved. Published in 2018 by Children's Press, an imprint of Scholastic Inc.
Printed in the United States of America 113

1 2 3 4 5 6 7 8 9 10 R 27 26 25 24 23 22 21 20 19 18

Lion dancer

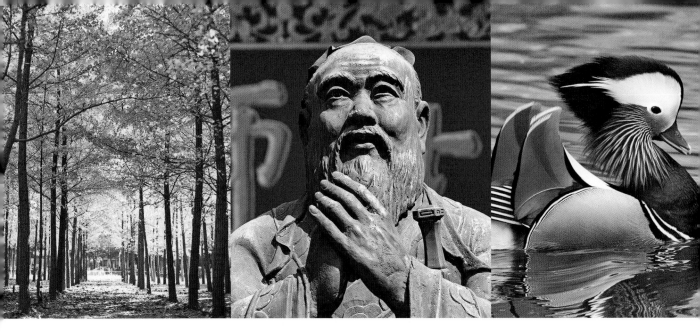

Contents

Left to right: **Autumn, Confucius, mandarin duck, Guangzhou, Zhuang woman**

CHAPTER 1

China
Today

8

FROM THE RICE FARMER IN LONGSHENG COUNTY TO the investment banker in Beijing to the electronics factory worker in Guangzhou, twenty-first-century China is a place of amazing contrasts.

China—officially called the People's Republic of China—is a land famous for its diversity. This diversity is most evident in the country's physical landscape. Stretching across most of eastern Asia, China has a remarkable variety of landforms. They range from frozen tundra to tropical forests and from fertile plains to towering snowcapped mountains to vast deserts.

The third-largest nation in the world in area, after Russia and Canada, China is home to roughly 1.4 billion people. With nearly 20 percent of the total world population, China is the most heavily populated country on Earth. Its people belong to fifty-six officially recognized ethnic groups.

Opposite: **Colorful signs illuminate the streets in Shanghai, the largest city in China.**

A woman passes by a silk shop in southern China. Silk, which is made from the cocoons of silkworm caterpillars, was invented in China.

China has one of the world's oldest civilizations. The first of numerous Chinese dynasties emerged about 2000 BCE. For centuries, powerful emperors ruled the land. The stability they brought to China fostered the development of important technological and social advancements. Paper, gunpowder, silk, and the compass are all notable inventions made by the engineers and scientists of ancient China. Great Chinese thinkers and artisans made significant contributions in philosophy, literature, poetry, and art.

Though China dominated Asia for nearly two thousand years, it shielded itself from contact with foreigners and the outside world for much of its history. By the late nineteenth

century, however, Western powers, traders, and missionaries had established a strong presence in China. The Chinese struggled to incorporate Western learning and technology into their culture, while preserving centuries'-old Chinese values. Ideas such as democracy took root in China, especially among the young. Internal discontent with the monarchy was widespread, and by 1911, rebellion and revolt overthrew the dynasty system in China. The new government was called the Republic of China.

In China, the family name is typically written first and the given name second, the opposite of how they are written in the West. The family name of the longtime Chinese leader Mao Zedong was "Mao." His father was named Mao Yichang. "Zedong" was Mao's given name, what Americans call the "first name."

Mao Zedong (center) led China for more than a quarter century.

In 1949, the new government was replaced with a communist government, the People's Republic of China. Mao Zedong, the country's new leader, helped modernize China,

Girls in Guizhou Province, in southern China

but his actions also resulted in famine and civil war, bringing great misery to the population.

Economic reforms introduced in the late 1970s launched tremendous growth in China. Today, China boasts the second-largest economy in the world, behind the United States, and in 2013 it became the world's largest manufacturer.

As the nation continues to modernize, China's leaders seek to solve major problems such as rural poverty, pollution, and overpopulation. Despite such challenges, the Chinese people welcome the future with hope and determination.

CHAPTER 2

Land of Contrasts

CHINA IS ONE OF THE WORLD'S LARGEST COUNTRIES. It covers more land than the continent of Australia and is nearly as large as Europe. The vast land stretches 3,100 miles (5,000 kilometers) from north to south and 3,400 miles (5,500 km) from east to west.

China is bordered by fourteen countries: Russia and Mongolia to the north; North Korea to the east; Vietnam, Laos, Myanmar, India, Bhutan, and Nepal to the south; and Pakistan, Afghanistan, Tajikistan, Kyrgyzstan, and Kazakhstan to the west. The nation also has a long coastline, which runs roughly 8,700 miles (14,000 km), fronting the Yellow Sea and the East China Sea in the east and the South China Sea in the southeast. Chinese territory includes more than five thousand islands, including the large island of Taiwan, off the east coast.

Opposite: **Jagged karst hills rise in southern China. Karst is made from limestone, which erodes easily, forming dramatic spires and cave-pocked land.**

The peaks of the Himalayas tower above the clouds along the border between China and Nepal.

Mountains, Deserts, and Plains

Within China's vast area lies a wide variety of landscapes that can be both spectacular and foreboding. The Plateau of Tibet, also called the Tibetan Highlands, is located in China's southwestern region. It consists mainly of hilly lands and towering mountains. The northern portion of the plateau has many lakes. Several rivers, including the Yangtze and the Yellow, begin in the Tibetan Highlands. Barren and frigid most of the year, the region is the least populated part of China.

The Himalayas, a large mountain system lying south of the highlands, is home to the highest point on Earth: Mount Everest. It soars an astonishing 29,035 feet (8,850 meters) above sea level—that's about five and a half miles high.

Farther north, the Xinjiang-Mongolian Uplands occupy the northwestern region of China. This mountainous area contains the Taklimakan, one of the world's driest deserts and part of the Gobi Desert. The Turpan Depression, north of the Taklimakan, is an arid basin that is the lowest point in China.

Stretching from the Gobi Desert into the northeast are the Mongolian Border Uplands. The northern part of the region is rugged, mountainous, and largely unpopulated. The Loess Plateau in the eastern portion of the uplands has fine-grained yellowish-brown soil called loess. In some areas, layers of loess can reach a thickness of 260 feet (80 m).

The Gobi Desert stretches for 1,000 miles (1,600 km) across China and Mongolia. Some of it is covered with sand dunes, and some with rock.

China's Geographic Features

Area: 3,692,260 square miles (9,562,910 sq km)

Highest Elevation: Mount Everest, 29,035 feet (8,850 m) above sea level

Lowest Elevation: Ayding Lake within the Turpan Depression, 505 feet (154 m) below sea level

Longest River: Yangtze, 3,915 miles (6,300 km)

Largest Lake: Qinghai Lake, 1,790 square miles (4,635 sq km)

Highest Average Temperature: Fuzhou, with average July highs of about 92°F (33°C)

Lowest Average Temperature: Mohe County, with average January lows of −21.6°F (−29.8°C)

Highest Average Annual Rainfall: Mount Emei, 322 inches (818 cm)

Lowest Average Annual Precipitation: Turpan Depression, 0.6 inches (1.5 cm)

Highest Recorded Temperature: Ayding Lake, 122.5°F (50.3°C), July 24, 2015

Lowest Recorded Temperature: Mohe County, −72°F (−58°C), February 13, 1969

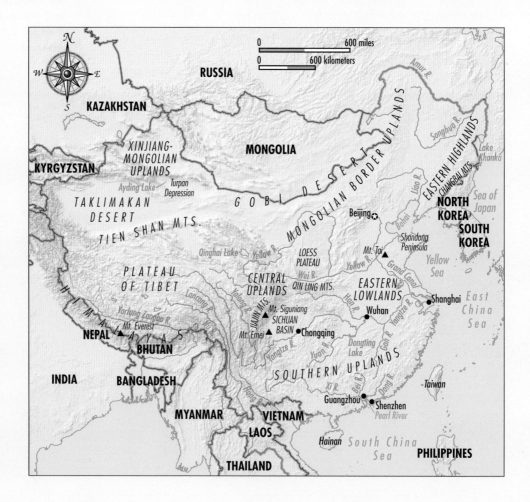

The Eastern Highlands consist of the Shandong Peninsula and eastern Manchuria. The hilly, rocky peninsula area contains some of China's finest ports. It also has large deposits of gold and iron ore. Eastern Manchuria boasts thick forests, providing the country with its best timber. The Changbai Mountains in the northeast form China's border with North Korea. The Amur River in the north separates China from Russia.

The Eastern Lowlands occupy China's eastern coastline and spread westward. The valleys of the Yellow and Yangtze Rivers are located in the lowlands, providing China with its best farmland. The lowlands are home to some of the nation's largest cities, including Shanghai and the capital city, Beijing.

Many fast-flowing rivers tumble through the Changbai Mountains.

Deadly Quakes

Earthquakes occur throughout the world, but when they happen in China the destruction and loss of lives is often catastrophic. The two deadliest earthquakes in recorded history occurred in China. In 1556, an earthquake rocked the Shaanxi Province in central-eastern China, killing more than 830,000 people. As many as 655,000 people died when an earthquake struck Tangshan in the northeast in 1976. Earthquakes in China's eastern regions are often especially devastating because roughly 90 percent of China's 1.4 billion people live in the eastern part of the country.

The Central Uplands occupy the region between the Eastern Lowlands and the Tibetan Highlands. The region's outstanding physical feature is the Qin Ling Mountains, which run from east to west.

The densely populated Sichuan Basin lies south of the Central Uplands. The region is protected from extreme climates by the surrounding high mountains and plateaus. Sichuan Basin is one of China's most productive agricultural regions, particularly for growing rice.

The Southern Uplands cover the entire southeastern region of China. Green hills and mountains mark this warm area. The Xi River and the Pearl River provide excellent transportation routes for southern China. Many of the nation's largest cities, including Guangzhou and Hong Kong, are located at the delta of the Pearl River. The oval-shaped tropical island of Hainan has dozens of rivers and streams that flow from its central mountains to Hainan's long coastline.

Rivers and Lakes

China has more than fifty thousand rivers. The most important, the Yangtze, Yellow, and Xi, originate in the western highlands and flow eastward toward the Pacific Ocean.

At 3,915 miles (6,300 km) long, the Yangtze River is China's longest river and the third-longest in the world. Rising in Qinghai, the Yangtze is one of the world's busiest waterways. It has served as an important transportation and trade route for centuries. More than seven hundred tributaries feed the river. Along its path, the Yangtze cuts through

The Yangtze is the world's third-longest river, trailing only the Amazon of South America and the Nile of Africa.

hundreds of miles of canyons and underground caverns before emptying into the East China Sea. The waters of the Yangtze River are used to irrigate wheat fields in the north and rice farms in the south. Flooding along the river is a major problem. In 1931 a flood killed more than three hundred thousand people and left forty million more homeless. It was one of the deadliest natural disasters ever recorded.

The 3,395-mile-long (5,464 km) Yellow River rises in the north central province of Qinghai. It sweeps northeastward and then turns south to empty in the Bohai and Yellow Seas. The

When the Yangtze River overflowed its banks in 1931, the city now called Wuhan was flooded. Wuhan remained underwater for more than four months.

river gets its name from the yellow-colored loess sediment that it carries downstream. Wind blows the fine, powdery soil into the river as it snakes its way through the northern provinces.

Over the centuries, the loess in the Yellow River has raised the riverbed more than 12 feet (3.7 m). During heavy rains, the river's banks cannot contain the excess water, so flooding occurs, often bursting through the dikes and levees built to prevent floods. The Yellow River has been called China's Sorrow because of the hardships the flooding has caused people of the region. Loess, however, makes the waters of the Yellow River highly fertile. Northern farmers divert the river's waters and use them to irrigate their crops, notably cotton, wheat, and corn.

The land in the Loess Plateau erodes easily, so farmers create flat sections called terraces on which to grow their crops.

A fisher steers his boat across Shuanglong Lake in central China.

The 1,216-mile (1,957 km) Xi River flows eastward in southeastern China to join the Dong and Bei Rivers south of Guangzhou. The three rivers form the Pearl River, which empties into the South China Sea at the port city of Hong Kong. The Xi is the major commercial waterway of south China, linking large southeastern coastal cities to the interior.

China has nearly twenty-five thousand lakes. Most of the country's freshwater lakes are located in the east, and most of its saltwater lakes lie in the west. Dongting Lake in Hunan Province in the southeast is the largest freshwater lake. The lake is fed by floodwaters of the Yangtze River in the months of July to September. During this period, the lake's surface area may increase from about 1,000 square miles (2,600 sq km) to roughly 7,000 square miles (18,130 sq km). In recent years, the lake has been overfished, resulting in the disappearance of numerous fish species.

Lake Qinghai in central China is the country's largest saltwater lake, with a surface area of 1,790 square miles (4,635 sq km). The lake is a popular tourist destination for biking and bird-watching. Over the last few decades, the lake has been shrinking. Several hundred square miles of its area have been lost and the surface level has dropped. Scientists believe the cause may be overgrazing in the region. Sand blowing into the lake from surrounding overgrazed lands has formed large dunes in the lake. In time, the lake may be separated in two.

Dirty Air

Many parts of China have dangerously high levels of air pollution. The main cause of this pollution is rapid industrial development. The pollution emitted by automobiles, coal-fired power plants, and steel and concrete plants are harming public health. Health officials estimate air pollution in some parts of China shortens people's lives by about five and a half years. From 2008 to 2015, the daily air quality in Beijing was rated unhealthy or hazardous two-thirds of the time. The situation got so bad in December 2015 that Beijing closed schools and factories to keep people indoors, and ordered half of all cars off the road for nearly a week.

To deal with the problem, China has begun to reduce the amount of coal that it burns in power plants and factories. Instead, it is encouraging the use of clean-burning natural gas and renewable energy sources such as solar power and wind power. The Chinese government is also enforcing regulations that were previously ignored, shut-

ting down or fining polluting factories. In addition, Beijing limits the number of cars that can be on the road on any given day. As more people demand cleaner air, progress is slowly occurring.

Climate

The climate of China varies tremendously from region to region. The different climates range from subarctic in the north to that of highlands in central China to subtropical and tropical in the south. Heilongjiang Province in the extreme northeast has long, bitter winters with average temperatures of –24 to 5 degrees Fahrenheit (–31 to –15 degrees Celsius) in January. Summers are short but warm, with temperatures averaging 64 to 73°F (18 to 23°C) in July.

Temperatures in the deserts of northern China range from highs above 100°F (38°C) in the summer to well below freezing during the winter.

A family admires towers made of snow at the ice and snow festival in Harbin, in Heilongjiang Province. In this frigid region, snow often remains on the ground for half the year.

The provinces in central China have short, mild winters and long, hot, humid summers, with average temperatures of 30°F (–1°C) in winter and 80°F (27°C) in summer. Along the vast basins of the Yellow and Yangtze Rivers in eastern China, the climate is temperate, with wet, hot summers and dry, cool winters. In China's rugged southwest mountain and valley regions, climate depends largely on elevation.

Southeastern China features hot and humid conditions. The coldest months in the city of Haikou, on the island of Hainan in the South China Sea, are January and February when temperatures are an enjoyable 60 to 72°F (16 to 22°C). During the hottest month of July, temperatures rise to an average of 92°F (33°C) and fall to only 78°F (26°C) at night.

Rainfall levels in China also vary dramatically from region to region, generally decreasing as one moves farther to the north and west. Some areas along the southeastern coast receive more than 80 inches (200 centimeters) of rain yearly. The Yangtze River Valley receives about 45 inches (115 cm). Farther north, the Yellow River Valley receives about 35 inches (90 cm). Annual rainfall in the northwestern provinces drops to as low as 3.5 inches (9 cm) in Gansu and 1 inch

Rain is common throughout much of eastern and southern China.

Trees bend and break during a typhoon in southeastern China. More typhoons strike China than any other country.

(2.5 cm) in parts of Xinjiang. About 80 percent of the rain in China falls between May and October.

Seasonal winds, called monsoons, affect the climate and amount of rainfall various regions in China receive. In the fall and winter, these powerful gusts come from the frigid north, bringing cold, dry air that causes drops in temperatures and humidity. In the spring and summer, monsoons blow in from the south, bringing moist, warm air and large amounts of rainfall to southern China.

China sometimes experiences typhoons, strong rotating storms that start in the Pacific Ocean or the South China Sea. They make landfall on the southern and eastern coasts of China and can bring dangerously high winds and huge amounts of rainfall. In the Atlantic Ocean, typhoons are known as hurricanes. The main typhoon season in China is July through September.

Urban Giants

With a population of about 23 million people, Shanghai (right) is the largest city in China—and in the world. It lies on the Huangpu River, where the Yangtze River empties into the East China Sea. Once a fishing and textiles town, the city developed into a thriving commercial center in the mid-nineteenth century. Today, industry such as the manufacture of automobiles, electronics, and steel products contributes heavily to Shanghai's economy. Shanghai is also one of the leading financial centers in the world. The Bund waterfront area features rows of commercial buildings in Western-style architecture. The Pudong New Area is home to one of the region's tallest skyscrapers, the Oriental Pearl Tower. At 1,536 feet (468 m) tall, it is the highest observation deck in Asia. Breathtaking views of the city can also be seen from observatories on the 101-story Shanghai World Financial Center, built in 2008.

Beijing, the nation's capital, is its second-largest city, home to about 18 million people. The nation's third-largest city is Guangzhou (below left), which has a population of about 12.4 million people. It is located in southern China on the Pearl River. The city, originally called Panyu, was founded in 214 BCE. Over the centuries, it served as the capital city of three Chinese dynasties. Among the city's major landmarks is the Bright Filial Piety Temple, one of China's grandest temples, which dates back more than 1,700 years. Yuexiu Park and Baomo Garden showcase the natural beauty of Guangzhou. Automobiles, electronics, and chemicals are the city's main industries.

Located roughly 90 miles (145 km) southeast of Guangzhou is Shenzhen, China's fourth-largest city with a population of 12.3 million. Thirty years ago, Shenzhen was a small fishing village. In 1980, the city was named a Special Economic Zone to bolster industrial growth and encourage foreign investment. Since then, it has been transformed into a modern metropolis with new skyscrapers rising each year. Many of China's most successful high-tech companies are based in Shenzhen. Popular attractions include Safari Park and Happy Valley, a vast amusement and theme park.

CHAPTER 3

Nature's Offerings

CHINA'S DIVERSE ENVIRONMENTS ARE HOME TO an incredible variety of plant and animal life. Tens of thousands of plant species are found in China. Thousands more species of fish, birds, mammals, reptiles, and amphibians inhabit the land and skies of this vast country.

Plant Life

China's forests, wetlands, grasslands, deserts, and other habitats are home to roughly 32,000 species of plants—more than 10 percent of the world's total—and 2,800 species of trees.

The cold northern regions, including the extreme northeast, contain some of China's richest timberlands. Large tracts of conifer, or cone-bearing, trees cover the region, including larch, spruce, and Korean pine. Because of the larch's extremely hard wood and resistance to rotting, it is commonly used to make fences, posts, and roof shingles. Chinese ginseng, a plant used in medicines, grows on the forest floor.

Opposite: **Mandarin ducks are among the many duck species that are found in China. They are striking birds, with whisker-like feathers around their necks, and wings that end in golden tips and stand up like sails.**

The Beautiful Blossom

The plum blossom is one of the most popular flowers in China. The pink, red, or white blossoms emerge on plum trees each spring. The flowers measure about 1 inch (2.5 cm) in diameter and have a pleasant scent. More than three hundred species of plums grow in China, which produces by far the most plums of any country in the world. The fruit is used to make juice, wine, and sauces, and is an ingredient in traditional Chinese medicine.

Deciduous forests—those with trees that lose their leaves in the fall—are typically found in temperate central China and include species such as oak, ash, and maple. Moving south-

Bamboo towers tall like trees, but it is actually a type of grass.

ward, bamboo and ginkgo grow in China's subtropical regions. Sea hibiscus and Chinese persimmon thrive in China's lush, tropical regions. These southernmost regions contain forests of mangroves, small trees with long, fingerlike roots that grow along the coast. Mangrove forests are important ecosystems. In addition to protecting shorelines from damaging storms and waves, they serve as breeding grounds and homes for sea life and migrating birds.

Plant life in the deserts of northwestern China is adapted to the harsh, arid climate of the region. Shrubs include the weedlike gray sparrow's saltwort, sagebrush, and hair moss. Saxaul is a nearly leafless woody shrub that grows about 10 feet (3 m) tall. It plays a critical role in the desert because its roots help bind the soil together and prevent erosion. Forests of saxaul also provide breeding grounds for the region's wildlife.

The Ginkgo Tree

The ginkgo tree, also known as the maidenhair tree, is native to China. Fossils of the tree date back more than 270 million years, making it the oldest living tree species. Today, this species of tough, hardy trees is grown throughout the world. Ginkgoes can live as long as a thousand years. They normally grow about 115 feet (35 m) tall, but some reach heights of 160 feet (50 m). The dried leaves of the ginkgo are used in medicines that treat a variety of diseases and ailments. For centuries, people have used ginkgo to treat blood disorders and depression, and to improve vision and memory.

Diversity of Life

China is home to a dazzling variety of animal life that includes more than 500 species of mammals, 1,300 bird species, 2,800 fish species, and 700 species of reptiles and amphibians. China is a showcase of creatures of all kinds: mammals such as gibbons, bears, antelope, beavers, and seals; meat-eaters including snow leopards, tigers, and crocodiles; flying creatures such as cranes, pheasants, and bats; and countless sea creatures, including whales, dolphins, tuna, and clams. Many species of wildlife are endemic to China, meaning they are found only there. Among

Yaks cross a river in western China. These shaggy beasts live in high, cold regions, where their hair keeps them warm, even at temperatures of –40°F (–40°C).

them are the giant panda, the snub-nosed monkey, the rusty-throated parrotbill, and the Chinese paddlefish.

The cold northeast region of China is home to reindeer, Siberian musk deer, gazelles, bears, and Chinese gorals, small goatlike mammals. Yaks, goats, and dzos—a cross between a yak and a cow—live in the chilly areas of the Xinjiang and Tibet Autonomous Regions in the far west. The south-central forests of China are home to the giant panda, one of the world's most beloved creatures.

Gibbons, macaques, and snub-nosed monkeys make their home in China's tropical southern forest regions. The island of Hainan hosts many varieties of wildlife, including fruit bats, crab-eating mongoose, flying squirrels, and sambar deer. The

Golden snub-nosed monkeys live in west-central China. Babies of the species are white or light gray. As they get older, they turn golden.

The Giant Panda

The animal most closely associated with China is the giant panda, the adorable member of the bear family with distinctive black-and-white markings. The panda lives high in the dense bamboo forests of south-central China, mainly in Sichuan Province. Adults measure 4 to 6 feet long (1.2 to 1.8 m) and stand 2 to 3 feet (60 to 90 cm) tall at the shoulder. Pandas feed almost exclusively on bamboo shoots and leaves, but they also occasionally eat fish or other plants. Long considered a symbol of peace in China, the generally shy, calm panda can act aggressively toward humans, especially if it is feeling threatened. Human activity, such as deforestation and farming, has significantly reduced the number of pandas in China. It is believed that only two to three thousand pandas remain in the wild. Visitors can see pandas in their natural habitat at sanctuaries in the Wolong National Nature Reserve, at Mount Siguniang, and at the Jiajin Mountains in Sichuan Province.

waters surrounding Hainan feature several species of whales, including baleen whales, humpback whales, and sperm whales.

One of China's most beautiful and rare mammals is the clouded leopard. It lives mainly in lowland tropical rain forests, south of the Yangtze River, but can be found as far west as the Himalayas. The clouded leopard is the smallest species of the big cats. It grows 4 to 6 feet (1.2 to 1.8 m) long, almost half of which is the tail. The especially long tail helps the animal balance as it climbs. The leopard is named for the cloud-like spots on its coat, which provide camouflage in the forest. Clouded leopards hunt small prey such as birds and

squirrels, as well as larger animals, including deer and wild pigs. Deforestation and hunting by humans threaten the long-term existence of these handsome animals.

High in a tree, a clouded leopard stands alert.

A Striking Bird

The red-crowned crane, also called the Manchurian crane, is one of the largest and rarest cranes in the world. It is the only crane species to have mostly white feathers, and its forehead and crown are covered with featherless, bright red skin. These handsome birds stand about 5 feet (1.5 m) tall with a wingspan up to 8 feet (2.4 m). In China, the crane breeds along rivers and marshes in the northeast, especially near Lake Khanka, a freshwater lake on the border of China and Russia. In the fall, the cranes migrate to the temperate climates of east-central China and Korea. Red-crowned cranes eat plants and meat, including parsley, carrots, acorns, and small mammals, as well as eels, carp, and other fish. The crane often appears in traditional Chinese myths and legends as a symbol of luck and longevity.

CHAPTER 4

An Inspiring Past

SCIENTISTS BELIEVE THE FORERUNNERS OF MODERN people lived in what is now northern China as long as 750,000 years ago. Fossils of these primitive humans, known as *Homo erectus*, were found near Beijing in 1927. These peoples were hunter-gatherers who used stone tools and made fire. Early *Homo sapiens*—the ancestors of today's humans—inhabited China about 200,000 years ago.

By 5000 BCE, people in China had learned to grow simple crops such as gourds and beans, and to raise horses, dogs, cattle, and pigs. People established villages along the banks of the Yellow River and in the delta region of the Yangtze River in southern China.

As the centuries passed, early Chinese society became more sophisticated. People developed systems of irrigation to help cultivate rice. They began crafting tools and jewelry from stones such as jade. By the fourth century BCE, the Chinese had invented the potter's wheel and mastered the complex art of making silk.

Opposite: **This hook in the shape of a dragon is decorated with jade and turquoise. Dating to the fourth century BCE, it would have been used to hold a robe closed.**

The First Use of Metal

The Bronze Age was the period when people learned how to mine and refine copper and tin to make bronze. It began at different times in different parts of the world. In China, the Bronze Age began before 3000 BCE, while in Great Britain it did not begin until 1900 BCE. Chinese bronze-working flourished during the Shang dynasty (ca. 1600–1046 BCE). Craftspeople made tools, weapons, and parts of chariots from bronze. Shang-era bronze drinking vessels, such as wine cups and goblets, were often decorated with finely detailed images of dragons, birds, and geometric patterns. In about 600 BCE, the Chinese began making objects with iron, ushering in the Iron Age in China.

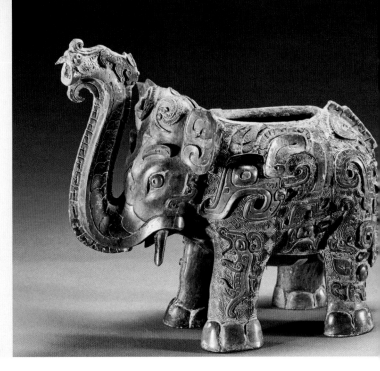

Early Dynasties

For nearly three thousand years, China was ruled by dynasties. A dynasty is a series of rulers who are all from the same family. During this time, China was sometimes united under one dynasty, but often competing dynasties from different regions struggled for control.

The Xia dynasty was the first ruling family of ancient China. The Xia lasted from about 2000 BCE until 1600 BCE, under the leadership of seventeen different emperors. Archaeological evidence indicates the Xia flourished in the Yellow River valley, near present-day Luoyang. During the Xia dynasty, Chinese people made objects from bronze, built dams and dikes to control floods, and created a calendar.

The Xia were overthrown by the second Chinese dynasty, the Shang, who ruled from about 1600 BCE to 1046 BCE.

Unearthing the Past

In 2011, archaeologists began excavating and exploring ancient ruins discovered about 12 miles (20 km) from the Yellow River in Shaanxi Province. After two years of intensive work, the scientists announced that they had unearthed the largest prehistoric city ruins ever found in China. Dating back to 2300 BCE, the Shimao Ruins cover an area of more than 5.5 square miles (14 sq km). Archaeologists discovered the remains of palaces, houses, tombs, and workshops. Murals, pottery shards, and jade objects uncovered at the site indicate Shimao was an important hub of northern Chinese culture. More than eighty skulls were discovered in two pits. They are believed to have belonged to people killed in sacrificial rituals.

The Shang were the first Chinese group to develop writing, and they left written records about their society on bronze vessels and on animal bones. The Shang built large cities with grand temples and palaces. They practiced town planning and developed the concept of money, using seashells as currency.

The Zhou, the longest-lasting Chinese dynasty, which reigned until 221 BCE, conquered the Shang. During the Zhou dynasty, China experienced rapid changes. Iron, coins, and written laws were introduced. New roads and canals were built, and trade with neighboring regions prospered. Great Chinese philosophers, such as Confucius and Laozi, flourished.

The Moral Life

Confucius, China's famous teacher and philosopher, was born in 551 BCE in what is present-day Shandong Province. He grew up in a poor but noble family and became a government worker in his teens. Confucius believed a society should behave with compassion, morality, and traditional values. He became a teacher, traveling widely through China spreading his ideology. The small following he gained blossomed into Confucianism, ideals that helped guide the Chinese for more than two thousand years. Although many people mistakenly believe Confucianism is a religion, it is actually a system of moral behavior.

Despite this progress, China under the Zhou was never fully unified. Local kings appointed by the royal family ruled kingdoms, or states, under the watchful eye of the Zhou king. In time, these kings began to pull away from the influence of the Zhou. In 770 BCE, some states rebelled, and the Zhou leaders were largely driven from power. Warring between several kingdoms raged for hundreds of years—until the real power of the Zhou dynasty finally reached its end.

The Qin Dynasty

The ultimate victor of the fighting was Ying Zheng, ruler of the state of Qin. Zheng established the Qin dynasty, which lasted only fifteen years, from 221 BCE to 206 BCE. Though short in duration, the Qin was one of the most important dynasties in Chinese history. Zheng renamed himself Shihuangdi, the "First Emperor," and is commonly known as Qin Shi Huang. He set about reuniting the fractured nation. He established a powerful central government, standardized Chinese writing, and developed a system of weights and measurements. Construction began on the Great Wall of China, and thousands of new roads, bridges, and canals were built to bolster communication. Under Qin Shi Huang's leadership, the level of China's education, culture, and commerce dramatically improved.

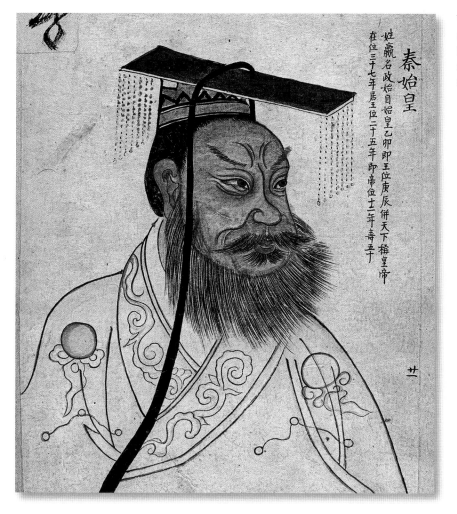

在位三十七年居王位二十五年即帝位十二年壽五十

姓嬴名政始目始皇乙卯即王位庚辰併天下稱皇帝

秦始皇

Ying Zheng became king of the Qin at age thirteen. By age thirty-eight, he had united China under the Qin dynasty.

The Great Wall

The Great Wall of China is one of the world's great technological marvels. Contrary to popular belief, the Great Wall is not a single wall but rather a system of walls, some of which run parallel to others. It is built with earth, clay bricks, and stone. In total, the Great Wall is about 13,100 miles (21,000 km) long. Some parts of the wall rise to about 30 feet (9 m). The structure crosses rivers, mountains, deserts, plateaus, and valleys. Its purpose was to protect China against invaders from the north.

Construction on the wall began in the third century BCE under Emperor Qin Shi Huang. The labor force was made up of soldiers, prisoners of war, convicts, and farmers. Few parts of these early walls remain. The largest and most enduring part of the wall was built during the Ming dynasty in the fifteenth century. The Ming wall alone is estimated to be about 5,500 miles long (8,850 km).

Archaeologists have discovered several unique features about the Great Wall. Glutinous rice, better known as sticky rice, was mixed into the mortar that was used to bind the stones together. The special mixture helps explain the wall's strength and endurance.

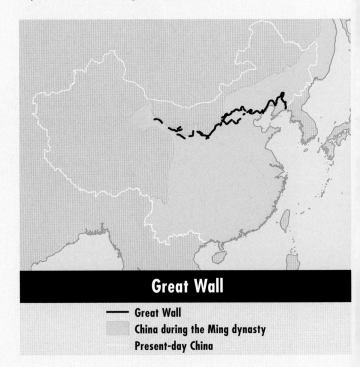

Great Wall

— Great Wall
China during the Ming dynasty
Present-day China

Qin Shi Huang unified China and maintained peace, but at a heavy cost: The new emperor was a brutal and ruthless leader. Qin Shi Huang killed off scholars who criticized his government and ordered that the writings of Confucius and other thinkers of the past be destroyed.

The Han and the Sui

The Han dynasty replaced the Qin and lasted for more than four hundred years, until 220 CE. During this time, Confucian scholars regained their importance, and Buddhism was introduced from India. Literature, art, and technology flourished. Paper was invented and an improved form of writing was introduced. Advancements in agriculture, such as crop rotation, increased the production of China's farmlands.

Prospective government workers had to pass special exams to ensure they were qualified for state jobs. Commerce with distant countries blossomed. As traders journeyed from China through Asia, the Middle East, Africa, and southern Europe, they established the ancient network of routes known as the Silk Road.

Following the Han, China dissolved into smaller, separate states that competed for control for more than four hundred years. During these unstable times, various dynasties rose and

Camels carried goods on the 4,000-mile (6,400 km) Silk Road across Asia.

Boats of the Sui emperor float on the Grand Canal in this eighteenth-century silk scroll.

fell from power. Confucianism began to decline. Buddhism spread widely in China, and a new school of thought, Daoism, gained a significant following.

China was reunified when the Sui dynasty came to power. This dynasty lasted only thirty-seven years, from 581 to 618, but the Sui reunified warring states and returned the country to relative stability. During these years, Emperor Wen began construction of a series of waterways that would later become the Grand Canal. This vital route linked north and south China, and is still used today. Eventually, costly and unsuccessful wars led to the collapse of the dynasty, and set the stage for the greatest Chinese dynasty, the Tang.

A ceramic tomb guardian figure from the 700s. Arts flourished during the Tang dynasty, including poetry, painting, and pottery.

The Tang Dynasty

The Tang dynasty, which lasted from 618 to 907, was a glorious age for Chinese culture. Outstanding Confucian scholars led the stable, well-organized government. Improvements to agriculture and increased trading along the Silk Road helped China's economy boom. Woodblock printing developed, and more books became available, which helped increase the population's literacy.

Traders, scholars, artists, diplomats, and missionaries flocked to China from Asia and Europe. These travelers brought with them new thinking and new religions, including Judaism, Christianity, and Islam. China itself grew as Tang armies conquered lands in central Asia, Korea, and parts of Vietnam.

Eventually, rebellion led to the collapse of the Tang dynasty. Once again China was thrown into chaos. The nation split into many parts.

Later Dynasties

From 907 to 960, five military dictatorships battled for control of China. Known as the Five Dynasties and Ten Kingdoms, these regimes desperately tried to reestablish the golden era of the Tang dynasty.

In 960, the Song dynasty emerged, beginning a period of great achievements and growth in technology and the arts. The invention of movable type simplified printing and reduced its cost. With movable type, printers could use type showing letters, characters, and other symbols over and over

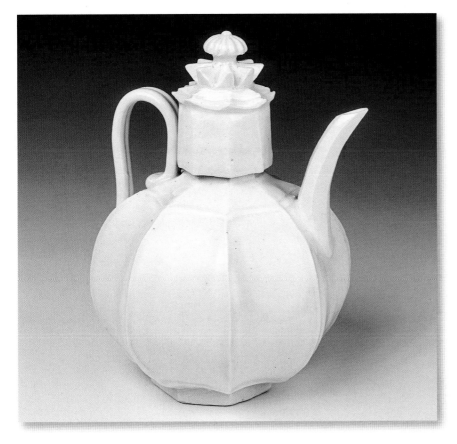

During the Song dynasty, pottery became especially delicate and graceful.

rather than having to carve a whole page at a time. This made it much easier to print documents and books, so literature and learning could spread farther. The newly formed central government introduced a welfare policy to assist the needy. Advancements in science and mathematics led to improved bridges and ships. Chinese artisans crafted beautiful glazed pottery and made handsome objects and jewelry of jade. Writers, poets, and musicians introduced new forms of Chinese creative expression.

By the late twelfth century, the Song dynasty began

In movable type, each piece of type is carved with a letter or character. The individual pieces are then lined up to form words and sentences, and secured in a frame to be printed. Movable type printing was developed in China about four hundred years before it was invented in Europe.

to decline. In 1211, the Mongols, led by Genghis Khan, attacked China from the north. The Mongols captured Beijing, and China fell under foreign rule for the first time. In 1279, Kublai Khan, grandson of Genghis, ousted the remaining Song leadership in the south and established the Yuan dynasty. Kublai opened China's doors to foreigners and appointed non-Chinese to important government positions.

The Ming dynasty ousted the Mongols in 1368, and ruled until 1644. Trade flourished once again, and Beijing was officially established as the nation's capital. Importantly, for the first time, Chinese leaders established diplomatic relations with Europeans.

China's last dynasty was the Qing, which began when Manchus from the north crossed the Great Wall and captured Beijing. Once again, China was under foreign control. The Qing ruled for 268 years, from 1644 until 1912. During this time, the empire expanded, as Tibet, Taiwan, and Xinjiang came under Manchu control.

Mongol Empire

Growth of the Mongol Empire, 1227–1259:
Mongol Empire, 1227
Lands added by 1241
Lands added by 1259
Present-day China

Foreign Involvement

By the 1850s, China's population was more than four hundred million. The nation was in debt and taxes were high. Poverty

An English merchant trades goods in Canton (now Guangzhou). For about a century beginning in the mid-1700s, Canton was the only Chinese port open to foreign trade.

and hunger became widespread. Meanwhile, foreign traders from Europe, the United States, and Japan arrived in China to buy tea, spices, silk, and manufactured goods. Wary of the Europeans, Qing rulers placed trade restrictions on the outsiders.

Foreign powers responded by dividing China into "spheres of influence," in which they each took control of certain parts of China. Hong Kong and the port of Shanghai fell to the British. The Germans controlled Shandong Province on the east coast. By 1900, Russia and Japan also claimed a piece of China.

Angry and bitter, Chinese rebels tried to drive out the newcomers. In an uprising known as the Boxer Rebellion, rebels burned down churches and massacred foreigners and

Chinese Christians. The Boxers, as the rebels were called, overran the foreigners' quarters in Beijing. Finally, an international force was sent to China to put down the uprising. The rebellion ended in 1901, and China was made to pay $330 million in damages to the foreigners.

By this time, armed revolutionary groups in China were working to oust the foreigners and replace the centuries'-old dynasty system of imperial rule with a republic. In 1911,

American marines march through Tianjin during the Boxer Rebellion. Forces from seven Western nations as well as Russia and Japan fought the rebels.

the last Qing ruler was forced from power. A new chapter in Chinese history was about to unfold.

The Chinese Republic

The Republic of China was established in 1912. Sun Yat-sen, the leader of China's Nationalist Party—the Kuomintang— became the nation's new president. But the nation was still not united. For more than a decade, powerful regional warlords battled to gain control of the country. When Sun died in 1925, Chiang Kai-shek took command of the party. Chiang believed in traditional government rule by a small group of leaders.

In 1921, people opposing the Kuomintang established the Chinese Communist Party under the leadership of Mao Zedong. The communists believed the government should

China's "Father"

Sun Yat-sen, the man known as the Father of the Nation, was the founder and leader of the Kuomintang, also known as the Nationalist Party of China. When the Mongol Qing dynasty was on the verge of collapse, Sun was elected provisional president of the newly formed Republic of China by a panel of delegates from China's provinces. Sun held that position briefly in early 1912 and then stepped down to organize a national assembly for the new government. Sun's republic was based on his Three Principles of the People: nationalism, the rights of the people, and the livelihood of the people.

control the economy. Despite their differences, however, the Kuomintang and communists joined forces to successfully crush the warlords.

In 1927, Chiang turned against his former communist allies, imprisoning or killing many. Those who escaped fled south to the mountains in Jiangxi Province. Mao reorganized his supporters and established communist control in the region. Chiang decided it was time to finally eliminate the communists for good.

In October 1934, Chiang's forces surrounded Mao's stronghold with about one million troops. Facing certain defeat, Mao led nearly one hundred thousand soldiers and Chinese Communist Party officials on a 6,000-mile (10,000 km) retreat from Jiangxi north to Shaanxi Province. This became known as the Long March. Only about eight thousand people survived the rugged trek. Along the way, many peasants and young people joined the communist cause.

In July 1937, Japan invaded China and seized control of the eastern provinces and most of the large cities. Unable to fight both Japan and Mao Zedong, Chiang renewed his alliance with the communists. When World War II (1939–1945) broke out, the Nationalists and the communists fought against the Japanese.

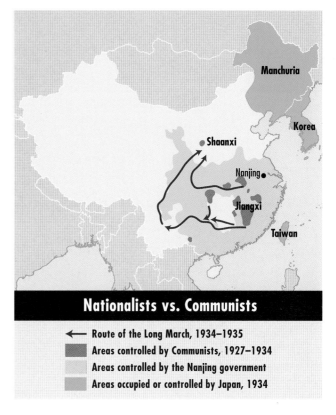

Nationalists vs. Communists

← Route of the Long March, 1934–1935
Areas controlled by Communists, 1927–1934
Areas controlled by the Nanjing government
Areas occupied or controlled by Japan, 1934

Mao Zedong addresses his followers during the Long March. By the end of the march, Mao had cemented his position as the leader of the Chinese communists.

The People's Republic of China

When World War II ended, Chiang and Mao resumed their rivalry. Civil war raged until 1949, when the communists seized control of Nanjing, the Nationalist capital. On October 1, 1949, Mao Zedong announced the establishment of the People's Republic of China. Chiang and the Nationalists fled to the island of Taiwan, where they continued the government of the Republic of China.

The new communist government banned private business and took control of important industries. It seized land from farmers and forced people to work in communes, where they farmed together in large groups. In the late 1950s, floods and bad harvests led to nationwide famine. An estimated forty million people died of hunger. It was the largest famine in human history. Opposition to Mao's leadership began to grow.

In 1966, Mao launched the Cultural Revolution to eliminate what he considered harmful elements in Chinese society. Scholars, scientists, artists and opposition political leaders were killed or put to hard labor. The movement lasted for ten years, until Mao's death in 1976.

Workers hold copies of Mao's Little Red Book, a compilation of his sayings about communism, government, and society. During the Cultural Revolution, most Chinese people were forced to own the book and were expected to accept Mao's ideas.

Recent Years

Deng Xiaoping became the leader of China in 1978. During his years as China's paramount leader, Deng instituted important economic and social reforms that helped modernize his nation. He opened up China to foreign trade and investment, and allowed more religious freedom.

Still, there were tensions. Political corruption was widespread, and in the 1980s, inflation soared out of control. Urban dwellers, especially college students, were dissatisfied. In 1989, students assembled in Tiananmen Square, a large plaza in the center of Beijing. The protesters had gathered to demand greater democracy and the end to corruption of communist officials. After weeks of heated protests, Chinese army troops fired on the protesters. Many hundreds were killed. Countries around the world criticized China for the massacre.

Since the time Deng stepped down from power in 1993, Jiang Zemin, Hu Jintao, and Xi Jinping have served as presidents of China. Under their leadership, the nation improved relations with other countries and achieved remarkable economic growth. An estimated six hundred million Chinese have risen out of poverty in the last four decades. Private enterprise and foreign investment and trade have boosted the economy to unprecedented heights. In 1997, China reacquired Hong Kong in a peaceful return from the United Kingdom.

Politically, the Chinese Communist Party rules with a firm hand, and government corruption continues to be a problem. In 2010, China had nearly 180,000 protests and mass demonstrations condemning government policies and widespread

corruption. China's leaders struggle with the wide gap in wealth between the country's rich and poor and with human rights reforms.

China has come a long way since its ancient beginnings. For centuries, the Chinese have endured dynastic rule, internal conflict, and foreign intervention. Today, the nation is a major player on the world stage—an economic, technological, and military superpower.

Hundreds of thousands of people gather in Tiananmen Square in 1989 to demand a say in their government. After several weeks, Chinese officials broke up the protests and declared martial law, sending hundreds of thousands of troops into Beijing to patrol the streets.

An Inspiring Past **59**

CHAPTER 5

A Single Ruling Party

SINCE 1949, THE CHINESE COMMUNIST PARTY (CCP) has ruled China. Under communism, the government typically owns the major resources of a country, such as factories and farms. People are expected to work for the benefit of the entire nation, rather than themselves. Wealth is distributed to the citizens based on the individual's need.

Politically, China is an authoritarian state governed by one party—the CCP. The party oversees all branches of the government, from the national level down to local levels. The leaders of nearly all government institutions are members of the CCP. Unlike the United States or Canada, where voters select their leaders in public elections, the Chinese system is based on appointment. The average citizen in China has little voice in his or her government.

Since the 1970s, the communist government has made small strides toward greater democracy in China. Today, all of China's one million villages hold free elections every three years for local representatives. However, critics claim even these local elections are influenced by CCP officials. Ultimately, until the CCP allows opposition political parties to exist, democracy in China will be impossible to attain.

A woman in Beijing casts her ballot for a local representative. Even these elections are dominated by the CCP.

China's National Government

EXECUTIVE BRANCH

President

Vice President

State Council

Ministers

LEGISLATIVE BRANCH

National People's Congress

JUDICIAL BRANCH

Supreme People's Court

Local People's Courts

Parts of the Government

The executive branch of China's government consists of the president, the vice president, and the State Council. The president is the official head of state, a position that is mainly ceremonial. The president receives foreign diplomats, ratifies treaties, appoints or removes high officials, and declares a state of war. The National People's Congress (NPC), the legislative part of the government, elects the president to a five-year term. A vice president is elected separately.

Xi Jinping is both the president of China and the leader of the Communist Party of China. The son of a high-ranking Chinese Communist Party leader, Xi Jinping joined the party in 1974 and rose quickly through its ranks. He studied agriculture in the United States in the 1980s and then returned to China. After serving in several government positions in different provinces and in Shanghai, he was elected vice president of China in 2008 and oversaw the final preparations for the Summer Olympics in Beijing. In March 2013, he was elected president of the People's Republic of China. Xi's vision for his nation, the "Chinese Dream," includes better education, higher income, and a cleaner environment.

The State Council, also known as the Central People's Government, holds the true executive power in China. It is made up of the premier, vice premiers, state councillors, and the secretary-general. The Chinese president nominates the premier, but the council itself wields final approval. The premier is the head of government in China and oversees the work of the State Council.

Nearly fifty different bureaus and ministries are part of the State Council, each responsible for an important aspect of Chinese society. Among them are the Ministry of National Defense, Ministry of Foreign Affairs, and State Commission of Ethnic Affairs. The premier nominates each minister, but the NPC must approve the appointment. One of the State Council's most critical responsibilities is managing China's budget and economic plans.

According to China's constitution, the National People's Congress, the nation's legislative branch, is "the highest organ of state power." It has the authority to make laws, amend the constitution, and remove government officials. The NPC has about three thousand deputies elected by smaller congresses in the provinces. The Chinese Communist Party greatly influences who is elected, and party members make up nearly all the leadership of the NPC.

Attendants serve tea to representatives of the National People's Congress.

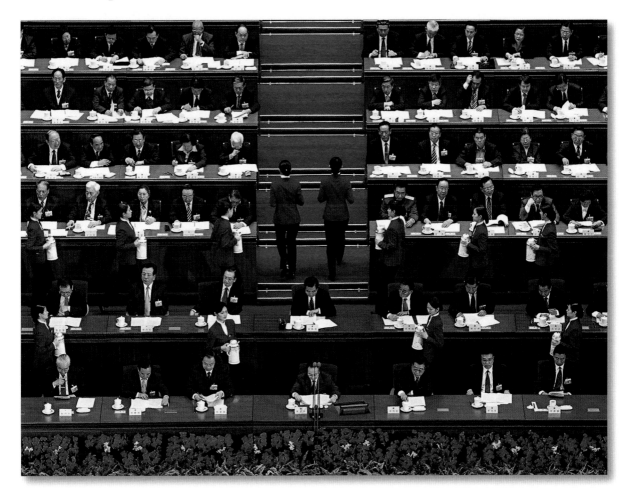

Justices on the Supreme People's Court serve five-year terms.

With so many deputies, the full NPC assembles only once a year for two weeks. A smaller group, the 150-member Standing Committee, meets regularly to approve new laws or deal with issues involving foreign nations.

The judicial branch of China's government is composed of the Supreme People's Court and the Local People's Courts. The Supreme People's Court, the highest in the nation, hears cases that most significantly affect national affairs. The three hundred or so judges of the Supreme People's Court are appointed by the NPC and report to that body as well.

The Local People's Courts operate at the provincial and local levels. These courts try minor and serious criminal cases.

The Special People's Courts hear cases involving military and transportation issues.

Administrative Divisions

To make for easier, more efficient governing, China is divided into smaller units: twenty-three provinces, five autonomous regions, four municipalities, and two special administrative regions, or SARs. Provinces are further divided into towns, cit-

Macau was under Portuguese control from 1557 to 1999. Today it is a special administrative region of China.

ies, and counties. China's five autonomous regions are Guangxi, Inner Mongolia, Ningxia, Xinjiang, and Tibet. These regions are composed of large numbers of minority ethnic groups. Limited self-government is allowed in these places. The four municipalities—Beijing, Chongqing, Shanghai, and Tianjin—are independent and report directly to the central government.

The two SARs—Hong Kong and Macau—are the former colonies of Great Britain and Portugal, respectively. These regions rejoined China in the late 1990s. SARs operate independently of Beijing under the slogan "One country, two systems." Each region has its own currency and elects its own assemblies.

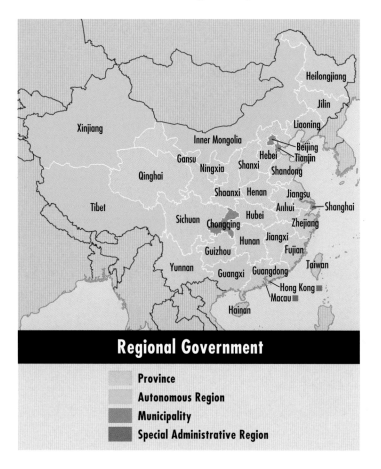

Regional Government

- Province
- Autonomous Region
- Municipality
- Special Administrative Region

Military

China has the world's largest military force with about 2.3 million frontline soldiers. The military is called the Chinese People's Liberation Army (PLA). It includes an army, a navy, an air force, and two special branches, the Rocket Force and the Strategic Support Force. By law, all Chinese citizens must serve in the military. However, because of China's large population and high number of volunteers, man-

The National Anthem

"March of the Volunteers" is the national anthem of China. The anthem was written by poet Tian Han in 1934 and set to music by Nie Er the following year. According to the Chinese government, the anthem may not be sung at weddings, parties, or funerals. Changing the melody or the words is forbidden.

English translation

Arise, ye who refuse to be slaves!
With our flesh and blood, let us build our new Great Wall!
The Chinese nationality has come to its time of greatest danger,
Each person must send out a final roar.
Arise! Arise! Arise!
Our great masses are of one heart,
Braving the enemy's gunfire, march on!
Braving the enemy's gunfire, march on!
March on! March on! On!

datory military service is not enforced. The PLA reports to the Central Military Commission of the Communist Party of China.

Foreign Affairs

Since the founding of the People's Republic of China in 1949, China's foreign policy has changed greatly. For many years, there was a lot of tension with other nations, such as the United States, that opposed communism. After Mao Zedong's death, however, China's leaders worked to improve relations with other nations.

A turning point in foreign policy came in the 1980s with the opening of China's economy to the world market. The Chinese government encouraged foreign investment and trade. This led to both warmer political relations with the world's major powers and tremendous economic growth.

Beijing, China's capital and second-largest city, is located in northern China, near the port city of Tianjin. It is home to roughly eighteen million people. Beijing was founded as the City of Ji more than three thousand years ago during the Zhou dynasty. In 1279, Kublai Khan, emperor of the Mongol-led Yuan dynasty, made Beijing the capital for the first time.

Beijing is a modern, bustling metropolis and the center of Chinese politics and culture. The city is divided into several districts. The Dongcheng District covers the eastern half of the city and is the most important tourist spot in Beijing. The Forbidden City (right), built between 1406 and 1420, served as the imperial palace for twenty-four emperors during the Ming and Qing dynasties. The palace complex consists of 980 buildings, surrounded by a 26-foot-high (8 m) defensive wall and

a 170-foot-wide (52 m) moat. Tiananmen Square, the site of the 1989 massacre of protesting students, and the Temple of Heaven, where emperors once prayed, is also located in Dongcheng. Other important sites in Beijing include the ancient cliff dwellings at Guyaju Caves, the Lugou Bridge, and the Ox Street Mosque, built in 996 for Muslim worshippers.

Beijing's economy is among the strongest and most developed in China. Unlike most major cities, agriculture plays an important part in its economy. Outside the city, networks of irrigation systems and reservoirs provide water to farms. Other industries important in Beijing include steel manufacturing, textiles, finance, and automobile manufacturing. Beijing's historic and cultural sites have made the city one of Asia's top tourist destinations.

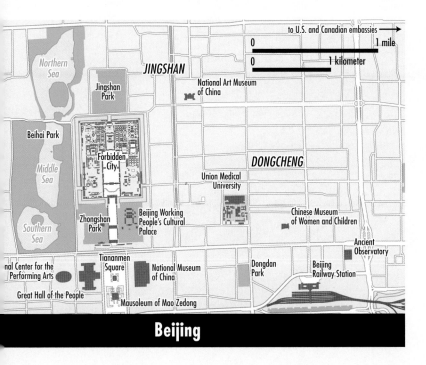

Beijing

CHAPTER 6

Economic Powerhouse

SINCE 1871, THE UNITED STATES HAS BEEN THE world's biggest economy. In recent years, however, China has threatened that number one ranking. In the last few decades, China's economy has grown at a rate of roughly 8 to 10 percent per year.

China's economic boom is due largely to the increase of privately owned businesses and foreign investment. In addition, the government has created special economic zones that produce only certain goods and services. Foreign investors receive business breaks, such as lower taxes, for investing in these zones.

Though China's remarkable growth has lifted tens of millions of Chinese out of poverty, many in the nation still face financial hardships. Poverty, especially among rural peasant farmers, still plagues China. It is estimated that roughly eighty-two million people in China live in poverty. Nearly seventy million Chinese workers earn an income of less than $400 each year.

Opposite: **Bundles of bamboo poles are moved at a construction site in Hong Kong. In China, bamboo is often used as scaffolding, the structure that workers stand on while constructing or repairing a building.**

Money Matters

The official currency of China is the renminbi, or "people's money." The basic unit of currency is the yuan. One yuan is broken into 10 jiao, and in turn, a jiao is subdivided into 10 fen. Paper bills come in values of 1, 5, 10, 20, 50, and 100 yuan, and 1, 2, and 5 fen. Coins appear in values of 1 yuan, 1 and 5 jiao, and 1, 2, and 5 fen.

Unlike paper money in the United States, Chinese money is brightly colored. Former Chinese leader Mao Zedong appears on the front of most bills, with famous national landmarks on the back. The 100-yuan bill shows the Great Hall of the People in Beijing; the 50-yuan shows the Potala Palace in Lhasa; and the 5-yuan shows Mount Tai in the Shandong Province. In 2017, 1 yuan equaled 15 U.S. cents, and 6.88 yuan equaled US$1.

The Young Nation Struggles

Upon taking power in 1949, the Chinese communists began remaking the new nation's economy. The government seized land from landholders and redistributed it to hundreds of thousands of peasants. By the early 1950s, the government had organized peasants into large cooperatives of about 250 families each. The people farmed the land they were given together.

The plan failed miserably. First, the plots of land were too small to produce bountiful crops. In addition, flooding destroyed much of the farmland. The result was a deadly famine that killed tens of millions of peasants. The situation worsened when Mao Zedong launched the Cultural Revolution in 1966. Millions of people were imprisoned and thousands more murdered by the state. Universities were shut down. The unstable political climate made it impossible for China to have a healthy economy.

After Mao's death, China's new leader, Deng Xiaoping, launched programs to put the nation on the road to recovery. Though the government still owned the land, peasant families were allowed to farm their plots and keep or sell portions of what they produced. Private ownership of small businesses was also allowed for the first time since the communists took power. Encouraged by their newfound opportunities, peasant farmers became more productive. Wheat and rice output rose dramatically. Farmers' income increased. As the years passed,

Men and women sell fruits and vegetables at a market in southern China.

As China has grown increasingly wealthy in recent decades, glittering skyscrapers have risen to fill cities such as Beijing.

private enterprise became a significant part of the nation's economy. Today, China has nearly six hundred billionaires—more than the United States has.

Weights and Measures

China uses two different systems of weights and measurements. Internationally, the Chinese use the metric system for weight, length, area, and other measurements. For more than two thousand years, however, the Chinese have used a separate system within their country. Weight is measured in *jin*. One jin weighs 1 pound (0.45 kilograms). Distance is measured in *chi* and *li*. One chi equals 13 inches (33 cm), and one li equals 0.31 miles (0.5 km).

What China Grows, Makes, and Mines

AGRICULTURE (2013)

Corn	217,830,000 metric tons
Rice	205,015,000 metric tons
Wheat	121,717,000 metric tons

MANUFACTURING (VALUE OF EXPORTS, 2015)

Computers	$188 billion
TVs and related equipment	$165 billion
Phones	$112 billion

MINING (2013)

Iron ore	1,320,000,000,000 metric tons
Zinc	5,000,000,000 metric tons
Lead	3,000,000,000 metric tons

The Chinese government began to accept loans and foreign investment. Deng toured the United States to demonstrate his desire to rejoin the international business world. In 1979, China created four Special Economic Zones (SEZs)—three in Guangdong Province and one in Fujian Province—to attract overseas monies. Foreign companies that set up businesses with Chinese firms in the SEZs were offered lower taxes and other benefits. Foreign investment poured in—and so did advanced Western technology and modern business techniques. Deng's policies resulted in rapid, never-before-seen economic growth. China is now poised to become the biggest economic powerhouse in the world.

China is the largest producer of steel in the world.

Manufacturing and Industry

Manufacturing accounts for about 45 percent of China's gross domestic product (GDP)—the total value of all the goods and services produced in the country—and roughly 23 percent of all manufactured goods in the world. The country makes thousands of consumer products, including clothing, shoes, toys, and electronics. China produces about 90 percent of the world's computers, 80 percent of air conditioners, and 70 percent of cell phones. As a major manufacturer of steel, China makes weapons, cars, trucks, planes, locomotives, and ships. Chemical manufacturing also plays a major role in China's economy. Nearly twenty-five thousand businesses produce fertilizers, paints and dyes, synthetic material, and other chemical-based products.

China boasts an abundance of natural resources, including those used for energy production. Petroleum deposits are located in the northeast and northwest. Oil accounts for about 20 percent of the energy in China. Natural gas can be found in Sichuan Province in south-central China. China is the world's largest producer of coal, and coal provides about 70 percent of the nation's energy. Reserves are spread throughout the northern and central regions. China's mines supply large amounts of iron, lead, zinc, cobalt, tungsten, nickel, and bauxite.

Agriculture

Once the center of China's economy, agriculture now makes up only 13 percent of the nation's GDP. The nation's agricultural production is the world's largest, yet only about 15 percent of its total land is arable. Some three hundred million Chinese work in the farming industry.

China is the world's leading producer of rice, which is grown mainly in the Yangtze River valley and in the southern provinces. Wheat, millet, and sorghum are grown in the cooler, drier regions of the north. Corn and soybeans

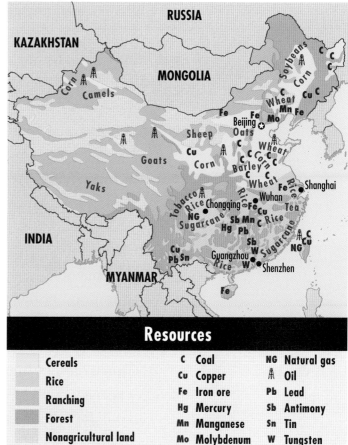

Resources

Cereals	C	Coal	NG	Natural gas
Rice	Cu	Copper		Oil
Ranching	Fe	Iron ore	Pb	Lead
Forest	Hg	Mercury	Sb	Antimony
	Mn	Manganese	Sn	Tin
Nonagricultural land	Mo	Molybdenum	W	Tungsten

are cultivated in both the north and the south. Other major food crops include tobacco, potatoes, peanuts, and tea. China is the world's leading producer of chickens, eggs, and pigs. Cattle-raising is done in western China in Tibet, Xinjiang, and Qinghai.

Since 1982, China has been the world's largest grower of cotton, accounting for more than 20 percent of all production. Cotton is grown in the Xinjiang Autonomous Region and the Yangtze River basin. More than ten million Chinese workers are employed in the cotton industry.

China is a major exporter of fish, though fishing accounts for only about 2 percent of the nation's total agricultural output. Most of the fishing occurs in the waters off China's east coast, particularly the South China Sea and the East China Sea. Inland waters provide a source of carp, catfish, eel, rainbow trout, and sturgeon.

Service Industries

Service industries employ roughly three hundred million people and account for half of China's GDP. A service industry provides a service, rather than manufacturing or growing a product. Some of China's largest service industries are health care, education, restaurants, hotels, and the government. Financial services, real estate, and even theme parks are growing segments of the service industry.

Tourism is one of China's leading service industries. Since the country opened its doors to the West in the late 1970s, China has become the third most visited nation in the world. In 1978, China welcomed about 230,000 foreign tourists. Today roughly

60 million international tourists visit China each year. Most tourists come from nearby South Korea, Japan, and Southeast Asia. About two million tourists come from the United States annually. China's natural beauty and historic sites are major attractions for the international and domestic tourist.

A worker lays out fish to dry in Hainan, in southern China.

Transportation

China's national transportation system has grown significantly in the post-Mao decades. Railroads are the nation's main means of travel. Railway lines total roughly 75,000 miles (120,000 km), the second-longest system in the world. About 40,000 miles (64,000 km), or about 60 percent, of the railroad network is electrified. The country's recently developed

The World's Richest Self-Made Woman

Zhou Qunfei, China's wealthiest woman, was born in 1970 to a poor family in Hunan Province. While working full-time as a migrant worker, she took courses at Shenzhen University, where she studied computer operations and accounting. In 1993, she started her own company with family members, making watch lenses. About ten years later, Zhou founded Lens Technology, a company that designs and manufactures touchscreens for computers and mobile phones. Today, the hugely successful company employs more than sixty thousand people at thirty-two different factories. In 2017, Zhou was worth $9.4 billion.

high-speed train service—with average speeds of more than 120 miles per hour (190 kph)—has been a boon to passenger travel in China. Roughly 2.4 billion passenger trips are taken on China's high-speed network each year.

In the mid-1940s, China had only 50,000 miles (80,000 km) of roads. Today, the country has roughly 2.8 million miles (4.5 million km) of roadways, including 76,000 miles (122,000 km) of highways, the most in the world. The Lianhuo Expressway is the longest continuous highway in China. The roadway stretches 2,600 miles (4,200 km), connecting Lianyungang in Jiangsu Province and Khorgas in the Xinjiang Autonomous Region.

With the overall rise in personal income, people in China are buying cars more than ever before. In 2015, roughly 250 million cars, including 136 million small-sized cars, were on the road. About 91 percent of the small cars were privately owned. In eleven cities—including Beijing, Shanghai, Shenzhen, and Tianjin—car ownership tops two million. Despite the huge boost in private car ownership, the bicycle remains an important means of transportation in the nation: More than 430 million Chinese own bicycles.

China has about five hundred airports of all sizes. The state-owned Beijing Capital International Airport is the nation's largest, and the second-busiest airport in the world. Beijing Capital carries about ninety million passengers each year. Air China, headquartered in Beijing, is China's largest airline.

China's high-speed bullet trains carry hundreds of millions of passengers every year.

CHAPTER 7

One Billion Plus

THE WORLD'S MOST POPULATED NATION, CHINA IS home to about 1.4 billion people, or one-fifth of the world's population. More than 90 percent of the Chinese population lives on less than 40 percent of the land. The heaviest concentration of people is in the central and eastern provinces.

China is filled with large cities. More than a hundred Chinese cities have a population greater than one million. Roughly 56 percent of China's population lives in cities. The number is growing daily: In 2014, the Chinese government announced it planned to relocate as many as 250 million people from rural farm regions to cities by the year 2026. The goal of the plan is to make farmers—who now grow their own food and provide their own energy—buyers of Chinese-made products and services. If successful, this plan will boost China's economy. If it fails, China may be faced with serious problems caused by further urban overcrowding and unemployment.

Opposite: **Nearly one out of every five people on earth is Chinese.**

A family in Shanghai, one of the world's largest cities

Population of Major Cities (2015 est.)

Shanghai	23,000,000
Beijing	18,079,000
Guangzhou	12,385,000
Shenzhen	12,337,000
Chongqing	11,054,000

Managing the Masses

By the late 1970s, China's population was quickly nearing one billion people. At the time, families had an average of five children each. Food shortages were widespread. The government feared it could not feed or educate the nation's children, or provide enough jobs for the adults. In 1979, officials introduced the one-child policy, in which many couples were forbidden to have more than one child. The policy, which was controversial, had an immediate impact on the swelling population. By the mid-1980s, China's birth rate dropped to three children per family, and by 2011, the rate fell to about 1.54. In 2016, the Chinese government revised the policy to allow all families to have two children.

Who Are the Chinese?

China is composed of fifty-six officially recognized ethnic groups. Nearly 92 percent come from one group, the Han. Their origins date back to the Han dynasty of 206 BCE to 220 CE. The Han live mainly in central and eastern China, along the Yellow, Yangtze, and Pearl Rivers. They are also scattered across the Tibetan Plain, and far north to Heilongjiang Province and south to the island of Hainan.

The remaining fifty-five ethnic groups make up about 8 percent of China's population. Most minority groups have their own language, customs, and religions.

A young woman at a market in Hong Kong. Most people in Hong Kong belong to the Han ethnic group.

A Zhuang woman in a traditional house

The Zhuang people, numbering about seventeen million, are the largest ethnic minority in southern China. They live primarily in the Autonomous Region of Guangxi.

The ten million Hui are Chinese Muslims whose ancestors came from Iran and central Asia between the seventh and the thirteenth centuries. The Hui live mainly in western China, and large numbers also live in Beijing.

For centuries, the Manchu lived in Manchuria, in extreme northeast China. In the mid-seventeenth century, the Manchu conquered China and established the Qin dynasty, which

lasted until 1912. Since the founding of the People's Republic of China, the Manchu have developed fishing and raising animals as their main livelihoods.

The Uyghur minority numbers about ten million people. They live mainly in the arid areas of the Xinjiang Autonomous Region in China's northwest, where they grow cotton and wheat. Many Uyghurs also live in urban centers, working in mining and manufacturing jobs. Ancestors of the Uyghurs gained distinction when they established a kingdom in north-central Mongolia in the third century. In the 1990s, large numbers of Han peoples moved into the Xinjiang Autonomous Region, which led to hostilities with the Uyghurs. Tensions between Han populations and China's ethnic minorities are not uncommon.

An Uyghur livestock merchant in Turpan, Xinjiang. China is home to the world's largest Uyghur population, but some Uyghurs also live in neighboring countries such as Kazakhstan.

A Vanishing People?

China's policy of forcing rural populations to relocate to cities and large villages might signal the end of some of the nation's ethnic minorities. For thousands of years, Tibetan nomads have grazed their livestock on the grasslands of the Tibetan Plateau. Since 2003, thousands of Tibetans have been moved to newly built villages across the plateau. But life is often difficult for the new settlers. The former herders do not have the skills to succeed in city jobs. Additionally, Tibetans face the risk of losing their language and cultural traditions. For example, Tibetan children are taught Mandarin instead of the Tibetan language in the village schools. Many other minority groups face similar problems that come with relocation.

With a population of less than five thousand, the Hezhe is one of China's smallest ethnic groups. For centuries, they have lived along the Amur and Songhua Rivers in Heilongjiang Province on the east coast. The Hezhe live on fishing and hunting, and wear clothes of fish and deerskin.

Language

Nearly three hundred languages are spoken in China. Roughly half of these are either rarely used or dying. Many different dialects, or variations, of the Chinese language are spoken throughout the nation. The official language of China is Mandarin. The form of Mandarin that is spoken in Beijing, called Putonghua, is the national language. More than 70 percent of Chinese people speak Putonghua.

Common Mandarin Chinese Phrases

Ni hao ma	How are you?
Wo xing . . .	My name is . . .
Zao an	Good morning
Wan an	Good evening
Xie xie	Thank you
Zhu ni hao yun	Good luck
Ni hao	Hello
Qing wen	Excuse me
Dui bu qi	Sorry

Mandarin uses about 1,300 different syllables, and most can be spoken using a different tone. In Chinese, the tone

Fish were central to traditional Hezhe culture and were used to make clothing, tools, and other goods. Today, some Hezhe people continue to use fish bones in their art and decorations.

that a speaker uses can change the meaning of the word. There are four tones:

- high and level, keeping the voice even across the entire syllable
- rising gently, as in English when asking, "Here?"
- falling and rising, as in asking, "May I . . .?"
- starts high but drops sharply, as in English when exclaiming "No!"

Chinese speakers must be careful to use the correct tone in conversation. For example, the word *ma* can have several

A teacher helps a child learn calligraphy. Traditionally, a brush pen made from animal hair was used to do Chinese calligraphy.

different meanings: "mother" (first tone), "to bother" (second tone), "horse" (third tone), or "to scold" (fourth tone).

The Chinese writing system does not have an alphabet. Instead, written Chinese is made up of about fifty-six thousand characters and symbols. The average Chinese writer and reader, however, needs to know about three thousand characters for everyday use. Each character represents a pronunciation, or sound, and a meaning. Some characters represent everyday objects. Others can stand for concepts, such as "up" and "down." Sometimes the same character has two or more meanings.

In 1956, the Chinese government introduced a form of simplified writing, which made characters easier to write and learn. The system was taught widely in schools and helped raise literacy levels throughout the country. The traditional form of writing is still used in Hong Kong, Macau, and Taiwan.

CHAPTER 8

Diverse Beliefs

FFICIALLY, THE CHINESE GOVERNMENT IS ATHEISTIC, meaning it does not encourage the practice of any religion. Historically, the state views religion as a threat to its authority. The constitution of the People's Republic of China claims, "The citizens of China enjoy freedom of religious belief." This statement, however, is not a guarantee for someone to worship as they want. The constitution also says that religious practices include only "normal religious activities"—without defining what "normal" means.

During the Cultural Revolution, houses of worship were often closed down or destroyed. Many religious leaders were arrested and sent to work camps. Since the early 1980s, the government has relaxed its policy toward religious worship and shown more tolerance of religious expression. Reports say the number of people practicing religion—and the number of temples, churches, and mosques—is growing.

Opposite: **One of Beijing's most notable buildings is the Daoist Temple of Heaven, which includes the Hall of Prayer for Good Harvests. Constructed in about 1420, the wooden building burned to the ground in the 1800s, but it was rebuilt in the same style as the original.**

In many Chinese temples, coiled incense hangs from the ceilings.

The government officially recognizes five religions: Buddhism, Daoism, Islam, Protestantism, and Catholicism. Most Chinese people practice a mixture of China's traditional belief systems of Daoism, Confucianism, Buddhism, and folk religions.

Daoism

Daoism teaches that people must live in harmony with the natural flow of the universe. The flow is called *dao*, or "the way." The dao is made up of two opposing forces: the yin (negative forces) and the yang (positive forces). To live in harmony with the universe, a person should perform good deeds, be tolerant, and not act selfishly. People should not be aggressive or overly ambitious, but instead be humble and reject material goods. Respect for the natural world and one's ancestors are also important beliefs of Daoism. The philosopher Laozi founded Daoism in the 6th century BCE.

Confucianism

A story is told that one day, a student of China's most famous teacher and philosopher, Confucius, asked the master, "Is there one word that should cover the whole duty of humankind?" Confucius replied, "Fellow-feeling is that word. Do not do to other people what you do not want them to do to you." This "golden rule" is the basis of Confucianism.

A New Threat to Religious Freedom?

In late 2016, the State Administration for Religious Affairs (SARA) of China announced a new law that could significantly limit freedom of religion throughout the country. The regulations order that SARA must approve all religious activities and places of worship, including private homes. Additionally, no religious material may be published and no donations can be made to a religious organization without SARA's approval.

Some people believe the new law specifically targets the practice of Christianity. In China, all religious groups and religious leaders must register with SARA. About twenty-five million Christians are registered at state-run churches where pastors are appointed by the government. But millions more worship privately in their homes, offices, and parks out of view of the state officials. It is these unregistered worshippers the government wants to control. Some experts believe by the year 2030, China will have the world's largest population of Christians.

Confucius is believed to have been born in Qufu, in Shandong Province in eastern China. The Temple of Confucius in Qufu is the site of many festivals in the philosopher's honor.

Confucianism teaches that having a good life on earth is achieved by having good relationships with others. Confucius taught several basic virtues: kindness, wisdom, courage, trustworthiness, and righteousness. He believed the citizens and government of a nation had a responsibility to act in an ethical way. Respect for one's parents, the elderly, and one's ancient ancestors were important for the well being of both the individual and society.

In recent years, the Chinese government has been promoting Confucianism. Around the world, the country has established hundreds of "Confucius Institutes," which teach Chinese language and culture. Additionally, government officials have attended conferences celebrating the life of Confucius. In January 2011, a large bronze statue of Confucius was unveiled at Tiananmen Square.

Buddhism

Buddhism is the third major religion practiced in China. It developed from the philosophies of Siddhartha Gautama, a teacher who lived in India between the sixth and fourth centuries BCE. He became known as the Buddha, or "Enlightened One."

Gautama was born into a wealthy family. In his late twenties, he left his privileged life and began to travel through India in search of personal happiness and contentment. He practiced meditation and came to believe that people could

Buddhist monks wear colorful robes.

Cave Carvings

Not far from the ancient city of Luoyang in central China, about 2,300 caves are carved into the limestone cliffs. Called the Luoyang Grottoes (small caves), the caves contain more than 110,000 Buddhist stone images and statues, and thousands of inscriptions carved on stone markers. The site is one of China's most important religious landmarks, and includes several large temples. A massive 55-foot-high (17 m) statue of Buddha surrounded by stone figures of monks and gods can be found in one of the caves. The grottoes were first carved during the Wei dynasty, more than a thousand years ago. Over the centuries the site was expanded and finally completed during the Song dynasty.

attain inner peace, or nirvana, by giving up their worldly goods and desires.

Indian traders brought Buddhism to China along the Silk Road. By the sixth century CE, the religion was firmly established in China. Buddhism teaches what is known as the Four Noble Truths:

1. Human life is full of suffering.
2. The cause of suffering is greed, desire, and ignorance.
3. One can achieve an end to suffering.
4. The way to end suffering is to follow the Middle Path. The steps of the path include meditation, helping others, doing useful things, showing compassion, and having good, wholesome thoughts.

Buddhists believe death is not the end of life. It is only the death of the physical body. The spirit will attach to a new body, and a new life. If a person was good in past lives, he or she will have enjoyable new lives. If a person led a bad life, he or she will have unpleasant new lives. Only by achieving nirvana can a soul escape the continual cycle of death and rebirth.

Chinese Mythology

Chinese myths were passed along orally for thousands of years before being written down in books such as *Shan Hai Jing* (Mountain and Sea Scroll). Many Chinese tales mix fact and fiction, and sometimes these are actually believed to be a factual retelling of history. Some myths borrow from the teachings of Confucianism, Daoism, and Buddhism. Common themes in Chinese mythology include the creation of the world, the importance of nature, and respect for ancestors. Many legends feature gods, and fantastic mythological creatures and places. Over time, elements of the myths have turned up in literature, music, dance, art, and architecture.

The Chinese Dragon

The Chinese dragon, or *long*, appears throughout Chinese mythology and the legends of other East Asian cultures. Most versions of the dragon are not evil as dragons commonly appear in Western culture. Instead, they are spiritual symbols, representing strength, nature, and even the magical. In ancient times, the dragon was often the symbol of the emperor in Chinese dynasties. In Chinese mythology, dragons are often associated with lightning and the coming of rain. To this day, Chinese farmers pray to dragons for rainfall for their crops.

CHAPTER 9

Proud Traditions

CHINA BOASTS ONE OF THE WORLD'S RICHEST traditions of innovation and artistic expression. Chinese contributions to the world of writing, art, and the performing arts are a great source of satisfaction for the Chinese people. In a speech given in Beijing in 2016, China's president Xi Jinping said, "Chinese culture's unmatched philosophy, wisdom, presence, and grace strengthen the innermost confidence and pride of Chinese citizens and the Chinese people."

Chinese writers, musicians, and others in the arts do not have complete freedom of creative expression. Censorship by the Communist Party often restricts the sale of books, movies, music, newspapers, and TV and radio broadcasts it believes threatens the government.

Opposite: **Traditional Chinese dance is graceful and elegant. The use of ribbons in formal dance dates back more than two thousand years.**

古原江山雪霽圖問羊道總論進
士天機秀于遠化井橫公所能企度後
于京卯見江乎常慶彩敢其幸慶六
梅相問余屏綠彷往追信久意致自外
圖諳老板客範法憶彷彷映自晚牛
戊中秋之石需夫人玉清彷此書自議

This painting by Wang Shimin accompanies the poem "Snow Over Mountains and Rivers." Like many Chinese painters from the 1600s, Wang Shimin focused on landscapes.

Chinese Arts

Chinese painting has traditionally focused mainly on nature and people's relationship with the environment. Landscape painting in China demonstrates the artist's desire to be part of the natural world, a world in balance and harmony. China's diverse geography—mountains, rivers, oceans, and deserts—frequently appears in Chinese art. Images of flowers, trees, birds, fish, and tigers are also commonly found in Chinese painting.

Traditional paintings, called *guo hua*, are usually done on delicate silk or paper made of rice or bamboo pulp. The artist uses a thick, pointed brush made of animal hair, usually wolf or sheep hair, dipped in black ink or colored dyes. The inks and dyes are made from a variety of materials, such as soot, minerals, or plants. There are two types of guo hua: *gongbi* features great attention to detail, and is used mainly for portraits, while *xie yi* is a loose, freehand style used in landscape painting.

Another traditional art form in China is called calligraphy. First practiced in China around 1700 BCE, the artist uses a brush and black ink to make ornate Chinese characters, the symbols used in Chinese writing. Some characters require as many as sixty-four brushstrokes to complete. Chinese paintings often include calligraphy. Painting based entirely on calligraphy is called *shuimohua*, or ink-wash painting.

Sculpture has long been an important art form in China. The earliest ancient Chinese sculptors worked with clay and stone. Around the seventh century CE, Chinese craftspeople began making porcelain, a type of glazed ceramic ware (made with clay) that is white and semitransparent. The highest-quality porcelain pieces were produced during the Ming dynasty. Known as Ming ware, these handsome blue-and-white porcelain pieces were exported to Europe in great quantity. They grew so popular in the West that they became known simply as "china." Bronze and jade were other mediums favored by Chinese sculptors. Though Chinese sculpting

Ai Weiwei is one of China's best-known modern artists. In 2010, he had a large exhibition in London, England, that included millions of sunflower seeds made from porcelain.

is most closely associated with green jade, artisans also worked with white, gray, and black jade.

Embroidery in China dates to the Zhou dynasty about 2,500 years ago. Ancient Chinese embroidery blossomed with the invention of spinning silk from silkworms. Both men and women have been involved in creating embroidery. Garments, shoes, eyeglass cases, furniture coverings, pillowcases, tablecloths, and different types of flags and banners were decorated with embroidery. Among the many themes featured on embroidered items are flowers, geometric patterns, landscapes, and animals, notably pandas.

The art of paper cutting in China dates back to the sixth century. Widely practiced today, this ancient handicraft requires only a piece of paper and a pair of scissors or a knife. Paper cuttings are used mainly to decorate walls, windows, mirrors, and other surfaces. They can be used to express emotions, such as joy and gratitude, or given as gifts during weddings and holiday celebrations. Years ago, cuttings of people or objects were buried with the dead in the belief they would travel with the deceased to another world.

A craftsperson displays a paper cutting depicting fish. Chinese artists often use red paper, because that color symbolizes happiness and good fortune.

Literature and Poetry

It is not certain when writing first appeared in China. However, historians know that by the time woodblock printing was used in about the seventh century CE, China had produced a large body of written works. The earliest literary works were myths and legends, often featuring ghosts and imaginary creatures. Beginning with the Tang dynasty (618–907 CE), the works of Confucius, Laozi, and other important thinkers were widely available.

Chinese writers produced many of the world's most important early works. The *I Ching* ("Book of Changes"), probably written around 900 BCE, teaches how to gain insight into the nature of the universe. It is still used by people to predict the future. Shen Kuo (1031–1095 CE) was an influential writer on scientific subjects. *Dream of Red Mansions*, written by Cao Xueqin (1715–1764), is widely considered one of China's literary masterpieces. First published in 1791, the novel sheds light on life in China during the eighteenth century.

Modern Chinese authors include novelist and short story writer Mo Yan. His major work, *Red Sorghum*, is set in the 1930s during China's civil wars and its battles with the Japanese. Mo won the 2012 Nobel Prize in Literature for his various works about Chinese folktales and history. Wang Anyi's *The Song of Everlasting Sorrow*, published in 1995, follows the life of a young Chinese girl from the 1940s through the turbulent years of the Cultural Revolution. The book established Wang, the daughter of the Chinese writer Ru Zhijuan, as a leading figure in modern Chinese literature.

The Poetry of Bai Juyi

Bai Juyi was one of ancient China's greatest poets. Born in 772 CE to a poor family, he nevertheless received a good education, and was writing poetry by the age of five. In about 800, he took a job with the government as a record-keeper. However, Bai got into trouble after writing poems that highlighted government corruption and the hardships of the common peasants. He managed to save his political career, and in later years served as a governor and a mayor in different regions. He was known as the Tang dynasty's "People's Poet." The following is an English translation of one of his most popular poems, "Feelings on Watching the Moon."

The times are hard: a year of famine has emptied the fields,
My brothers live abroad—scattered west and east.
Now fields and gardens are scarcely seen after the fighting,
Family members wander, scattered on the road.
Attached to shadows, like geese ten thousand li apart,
Or roots uplifted into September's autumn air.
We look together at the bright moon, and then the tears fall,
This night, our wish for home can make five places one.

Chinese poets also gained prominence during the Tang dynasty. Wang Wei was both a revered poet and an accomplished painter. It was said his poems contained a painting within them, and within the painting there was poetry. Bai Juyi wrote poetry and served as a government official. He is best known for his poem *Song of Eternal Sorrow*, which to this day is still taught in schools throughout China. One of the top modern poets is An Qi. Her work has been translated into several languages, including English and Hebrew.

Chinese opera is dramatic and stylized.

Performing Arts

Some forms of Chinese dance and theater date back to about 1000 BCE, when healers would dress in ornate costumes and sing and dance to music. Later, during the Tang dynasty, thousands of students enrolled in dance and acting schools. The Chinese theater developed gradually and blossomed during the fourteenth to seventeenth centuries. At that time, there were two main branches of Chinese theater: Liyuan Theater focused on the lives of the common people and was performed at marketplaces. Kunshan Theater was performed for the wealthy and the royal court. Much of traditional Chinese drama is based on the beliefs of Confucianism.

Jingxi, or Peking Opera, the most popular form of Chinese theater, first appeared in Beijing in the 1790s. A combination of elements from other types of musical theater in China, it has an energetic style that includes acrobatics, martial arts combat moves, and pantomime. Jingxi tells stories based on folk legends, classical novels, and other sources. Musicians playing wooden clappers, cymbals, fiddles, and flutes accompany the actors as they sing and perform. The performers dress in colorful costumes and headdresses, and wear bright makeup or bizarre masks. The National Center for the Performing Arts in Beijing is the leading showcase for musical theater in China.

Music

China has had a well-developed musical tradition that dates back as far as three thousand years. When performing traditional Chinese music, soloists or small groups play various stringed instruments, flutes, cymbals, and drums. The musical scale has five notes.

The seven-stringed *guqin* is one of the oldest known musical instruments played in China. Originally, the instrument had five strings—representing metal, wood, water, fire, and earth. Two strings were added later. Used mainly as a solo instrument, the guqin is plucked to produce a broad range of tones. The *dizi* is a flute made of bamboo. Simply constructed and easy to carry around, the instrument has been a favorite of both the Chinese common people and the upper classes. Some dizi are decorated with jade at both ends.

Over the centuries, different musical styles developed in different regions. In Fujian Province, Nanguan is a popular type of ballad. It is sung by a woman, accompanied by flute and a four-stringed instrument called a *pipa*. In Jiangnan, near the southern part of the Yangtze River delta, musicians perform *sizhu* (meaning "silk and bamboo") on stringed and woodwind instruments. Traditionally, the strings of the instruments were made from silk and the flutes were made from bamboo.

The guqin is one of the most respected Chinese instruments. Guqin players are often depicted in Chinese art.

Modern Chinese music features every musical style that can be found in Western nations: pop, rock, heavy metal, punk rock, electronica, and more. In recent years, Hanggai, a six-man folk group from Beijing, has blended Mongolian folk music with punk rock. Brain Failure, one of the few Chinese groups to sing in English, has toured the United States with other big-name punk bands. Queen Sea Big Shark, fronted by female lead singer Fu Han, is described by critics as "David Bowie-esque." Foxy Lady, the first all-female Chinese punk band, was an influential group that achieved success during the early 2000s.

Sports

Sports are a popular form of entertainment and relaxation in China. Modern sports began to appear in the early twentieth century with the establishment of the Republic of China. Most sports enjoyed in Western nations are played in China.

Both men and women play soccer on all levels, from schoolyard games to world competitions, including the Olympic Games. National Basketball Association (NBA) star Yao Ming, born in Shanghai, helped popularize the sport in his home country. Today, nearly three hundred million people watch basketball in China. The Chinese Basketball Association (CBA) is the top men's professional basketball league in Asia, with twenty teams in the league. The Women's Chinese Basketball Association is the women's professional league.

Basketball is by far the most popular team sport in China. Chinese people have been playing basketball since the late 1800s.

A Giant Among Men

Born in 1980 in Shanghai, Yao Ming rose to international stardom as a dominating player in the National Basketball Association (NBA) in the United States. Yao began his professional career in 1997 playing for the Shanghai Sharks of the Chinese Basketball Association. In 2002, he joined the NBA's Houston Rockets as a center. Standing 7 feet 6 inches (229 cm) tall, Yao was the league's most imposing player. He was named to the NBA All-Star team each year of his eight-year career and won the league scoring title in 2006 with an average of twenty-five points per game. Yao won three gold medals playing for China in the Asian Championships (2001, 2003, and 2005), and was named the Most Valuable Player of the championship each year. In 2016, Yao was elected to the Basketball Hall of Fame in Springfield, Massachusetts.

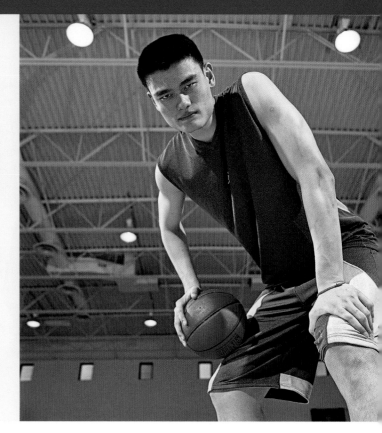

Tennis is a rapidly growing sport in China, played regularly by about fourteen million people. With about thirty thousand tennis courts nationwide, tennis has become the third-most popular sport in China, behind soccer and basketball. For nearly fifteen years, Li Na was the nation's top women's tennis star. Born in 1982 in Hubei Province, Li won nine World Tennis Association titles, including the prestigious French Open and Australian Open. Li Ting and Sun Tiantian won the women's doubles gold medal at the 2004 Athens Olympics.

China rules the sport of table tennis, known as *ping pang qiu* in China. Since about 1960, Chinese men and women players have dominated the annual World Table Tennis Championships, winning many medals in singles, doubles, and mixed doubles play. Since 1988, when table tennis became an Olympic Games sport, athletes from China have won twenty-eight of a possible thirty-two gold medals. Other popular sports in China include badminton, chess, swimming, and gymnastics.

The People's Republic of China hosted the 2008 Summer Olympics in Beijing. Chinese athletes won the most gold medals of any country, and placed second behind the United States in total medals won.

Li Xiaoxia takes aim at the ball during an Olympic table tennis match in 2016. Chinese table tennis players won every possible gold medal during the 2016 Olympics.

CHAPTER 10

Family, Food, and Fun

TODAY'S CHINA IS A FASCINATING BLEND OF OLD AND new. Towering skyscrapers, sprawling apartment developments, and modern homes can be found in every major city. Each day, high-speed commuter trains and subways carry millions of people to and from work in places like Beijing, Hong Kong, and Shenzhen. Yet in some regions, life is very different. In rural areas, people often live in mud-and-straw houses and farm with old, outdated tools and methods.

Regardless of where people live, socializing with family and friends is central to life in China. Chinese people tend to be loyal, polite, and respectful. Working hard and studying hard are traits that are taught to children at an early age. Importantly, equality between the sexes has generally become more accepted throughout the country.

Tasty Food

Chinese cooking uses most of the same basic ingredients found in Western culture. The difference is in the way the foods are

Opposite: **A mother and son ride a pedal sled across the ice in Harbin, in northeastern China.**

Egg Drop Soup

Egg drop soup is a popular everyday soup in China. It is delicious and easy to prepare. Have an adult help you with this recipe.

Ingredients

2 (14.5 ounce) cans chicken broth

1 tablespoon cornstarch

1 egg, lightly beaten

2 tablespoons chopped green onion

Directions

In a medium-sized pot, mix the chicken broth with the cornstarch. Slowly warm the mixture on a stove over medium heat, stirring frequently. Pour the beaten egg into the soup, and stir gently in order to break up the egg. Remove the soup from heat, divide into four bowls, and top with green onions. Enjoy!

prepared. Pork, chicken, and duck are popular meats used in Chinese cuisine. Rice is the staple food in southern China, and in the colder north, wheat is the staple. Meals in China are always accompanied with vegetables, ranging from spinach and broccoli to bean sprouts, watercress, carrots, and melon.

China's vastly different climates affect what can be grown there. Because of this, many of the foods used in cooking and their methods of preparation vary from region to region. In the northeast, wheat is used to make noodles, pancakes, and steamed buns and bread. Recipes feature onions, leeks, and

Chinese cooks have been making noodles for thousands of years. Traditional Chinese noodles are made by hand, pulled and twisted into long ropes.

garlic. Peking roast duck and dumplings filled with vegetables are favorites in the region. In the east, the region's rich, irrigated soil allows farmers to grow rice. The nearby oceans provide huge hauls of seafood.

The mild winters and fertile land of the southeast provide the widest variety of ingredients in all of China. Fruits, vegetables, and seafood are common. Buns filled with meat or seafood and sweetened with bean sauces or pastes is a favorite dish in the region. Southwestern cooking is known for its spicy hotness. Hot chili pepper and peppercorn are widely used in this cuisine.

A group of friends enjoys a meal of dumplings. Chinese people typically use chopsticks to pick up their food.

Some Chinese chefs light the oil on fire when frying to give the food extra flavor.

Meals are prepared in a variety of ways. Stir-frying is the most popular cooking method in China. The food is cut into bite-sized pieces and fried in oil. The food cooks quickly, keeping its tenderness and juiciness. Steaming foods in a bamboo steamer is another common method. It can be used to cook meats, seafood, chicken, vegetables, and dumplings. Ingredients are placed in the steamer, which is then fit snugly over a pot of boiling water. The heat of the steam cooks the food.

Mealtime

Most Chinese people eat three meals a day. Breakfast is usually eaten at 7:00 or 8:00 a.m., before schoolchildren and workers begin their day. The most common breakfast foods are porridge, steamed buns stuffed with meat or vegetables, noodles,

Catch the Dragon's Tail

Dragons play an important role in both ancient and modern Chinese culture. They symbolize positive values such as strength, wisdom, and good luck. Many Chinese children play a game based on these mythical creatures called Catch the Dragon's Tail. The game is best played outdoors with ten or more players. All the players stand in a straight line and place their hands on the shoulders of the player standing in front of them. The first in line is the head of the dragon, and the last in line is the tail. The dragon's head tries to catch the tail by leading the line around so that he or she can tag the tail player. The players in the line maneuver to keep the head from catching the tail. The line must not be broken: Everyone must keep their hands on the other's shoulders. When the head catches the tail, the player who was the head becomes the tail. All the other players move forward one position.

and soybean milk. Lunchtime is usually around noon, and features a meal of noodles or rice, and meat and vegetables.

Dinnertime is an important social event in the Chinese household because it is usually the only meal that the family enjoys together. It is also the biggest meal of the day. A typical family dinner consists of four dishes and a soup. Each person has his or her own bowl of rice or noodles. Serving plates or serving bowls filled with food are placed in the center of the table for sharing. The plates are never passed around. Using chopsticks, the person takes food from the serving plate and puts it directly into his or her bowl of rice. It is considered impolite to pass around the serving plates. Tea is drunk during the entire meal. Fruit is typically served at the end of the meal.

Housing

The People's Republic of China had more than 455 million households in 2012, more than any other nation in the world. (A household is defined as one or more people who live in the same dwelling.) The types of housing people live in vary dramatically in China, depending on the part of the country and the income level.

In large cities, most people live in state-owned apartments provided by the Chinese Communist Party. In a city such as Beijing, the apartment might have a balcony and large bedrooms. In the late 1990s, the government allowed private builders to create housing for the growing urban populations. Since then, the amount of urban living space has increased dramatically. Today, China's largest cities boast huge apartment complexes and newly built homes, which can sell for millions of dollars each. As the cost of housing skyrockets, however, millions of people are unable to afford a basic apartment in urban areas.

Many rural dwellers live in homes that are built around a courtyard, which may have plants and a small pond. Some families keep chickens or pigs in pens within the courtyard. Poor rural families often live in houses or huts made of wood, woven bamboo, or sun-dried straw-and-mud bricks. Many

Celebrating a New Arrival

The birth of a baby in China is a special occasion for both the newborn's family and the community. Most families hold a celebration on the thirtieth day after the baby's birth. On this day, the baby's head is shaved. The child is dressed in new clothes, usually red, as this is the color of happiness in Chinese culture. Relatives and friends gather at the parents' home to meet the baby. Gifts of food, such as hard-boiled eggs, cakes, chicken, ginger, and rice are given to the visitors. The eggs, which represent the new life, are usually dyed red.

Family, Food, and Fun **123**

homes have dirt floors and little furniture. Poverty in urban areas is a major problem. China's urban slums are home to nearly one hundred million people—nearly one-third the total number of people living in the United States.

Education

China's school system is the largest in the world. The system is composed of three parts: preschool, basic (elementary school, junior high school, and senior high school), and higher education. All children in China must attend school for at least nine years—six years of elementary school and three years of junior high school. Schooling during these nine years is free.

If students wish to continue their education after junior high school, they move onto senior high school or a vocational school to attend grades 10, 11, and 12. The tuition fees at senior high schools are high for the average Chinese family, roughly $800 a year. Students must pass a tough enrollment exam to enter senior high school. Upon graduation, students can apply to universities or seek jobs.

Celebrations

Every month of the year, Chinese people observe national or local celebrations and festivals. From the Ice and Snow Festival in January to the Hungry Ghost Festival in July to the Winter Solstice celebration in December, Chinese people enjoy celebrations year-round. The three major national holidays are known as the Festivals of the Living.

The Spring Festival, the first of the three major festivals,

Many Chinese schools require that students wear uniforms.

celebrates the Chinese New Year. It usually occurs between late January and early February. The holiday is preceded by a month of preparation in which families clean their homes and hang red decorations as symbols of good luck around the house. Children receive money in red envelopes and people dress in red clothes. On New Year's Eve, the family gathers for a special meal, called the Happy Family Reunion Dinner. Children living far from home travel many miles to rejoin their parents, siblings, and other family members. After dinner, the family sits together, eating snacks and playing games. As midnight approaches, fireworks are set off to "sound in" the new year. On New Year's Day, people dress in newly bought, brightly colored clothes to visit friends and relatives.

The Dragon Boat Festival, which falls in early to mid-June, is the second of the three Festivals of the Living. The festival is held to honor Qu Yuan, a great Chinese poet of the third

Confetti fills the air during a Chinese New Year celebration in Beijing.

century BCE. Qu drowned himself when soldiers of the Qin kingdom overran his state. When local villagers and fishermen learned the news, they rushed to the scene to rescue their revered poet. They climbed into their boats and searched the waters, but they could not find his body. Today, rowing races in boats decorated as dragons are held in honor of Qu's memory. The races are held on lakes and rivers in southern and central China. Spectators line the riverbanks to watch the dragon boats race and cheer on their favorite rowing team.

The Mid-Autumn Festival is the last of the three major Chinese celebrations. It usually falls in mid- to late September. The festival celebrates the moon, a symbol of harmony. At night, women fill plates with different fruits and place them on an altar near the family home as a "sacrifice" to the moon. The family gathers to gaze at the moon, play games, and eat mooncakes—

National Holidays

New Year's Day	January 1
Spring Festival/Chinese New Year	Late January or early February
Qingming Festival	April 4 or 5
International Labor Day	May 1
Dragon Boat Festival	Early to mid-June
Mid-Autumn Day	September or October
National Day	October 1

thin, sweet pastries filled with bean paste, lotus seed paste, meat, egg yolks, fruits, or nuts. People sometimes decorate with lanterns or burn incense. But the festival is mostly a time to gather with friends and family to admire the moon and enjoy their company.

Dragon boats vary in size, with sometimes dozens of paddlers, but they always have a drummer who pounds out the rhythm of the paddle strokes.

Timeline

CHINESE HISTORY

The first recorded Chinese dynasty, the Xia, forms.	ca. 2000 BCE
The Shang dynasty unites most of north-central China.	ca. 1600–1046 BCE
The Qin dynasty unites China; work begins on the Great Wall of China.	221–206 BCE
The Han dynasty begins rule as one of China's longest dynasties.	206 BCE
The Han state collapses; China breaks apart into smaller kingdoms.	220–589 CE
The Tang dynasty unites China for nearly three centuries.	618
Mongol leader Kublai Khan establishes the Yuan dynasty.	1279
The Ming dynasty overthrows the Mongols.	1368
The Manchu seize power and rule as Qing dynasty.	1644

WORLD HISTORY

ca. 2500 BCE	The Egyptians build the pyramids and the Sphinx in Giza.
ca. 563 BCE	The Buddha is born in India.
313 CE	The Roman emperor Constantine legalizes Christianity.
610	The Prophet Muhammad begins preaching a new religion called Islam.
1054	The Eastern (Orthodox) and Western (Roman Catholic) Churches break apart.
1095	The Crusades begin.
1215	King John seals the Magna Carta.
1300s	The Renaissance begins in Italy.
1347	The plague sweeps through Europe.
1453	Ottoman Turks capture Constantinople, conquering the Byzantine Empire.
1492	Columbus arrives in North America.
1500s	Reformers break away from the Catholic Church, and Protestantism is born.
1776	The U.S. Declaration of Independence is signed.
1789	The French Revolution begins.
1865	The American Civil War ends.

CHINESE HISTORY

The Boxer Rebellion seeks to drive out foreigners and reestablish traditional Chinese rule.	**1899–1901**
The Qing dynasty is overthrown; the Republic of China is founded.	**1912**
The Chinese Communist Party is formed.	**1921**
Nationalists and Communists struggle for control of China.	**1946–1949**
Communist leader Mao Zedong establishes the People's Republic of China; Nationalists led by Chiang Kai-shek flee to Taiwan.	**1949**
Tens of millions of people die during a famine.	**Late 1950s**
Mao Zedong launches the Cultural Revolution.	**1966**
Deng Xiaoping takes power and economic reforms begin.	**1978**
China adopts a one-child policy for most families.	**1979**
China adopts a new constitution, which gives people more rights.	**1982**
The Chinese army kills hundreds of protesters in Tiananmen Square.	**1989**
Hong Kong reverts to Chinese control.	**1997**
The Summer Olympics are held in Beijing.	**2008**
China revises its family policy to allow two children.	**2016**

WORLD HISTORY

1879	The first practical lightbulb is invented.
1914	World War I begins.
1917	The Bolshevik Revolution brings communism to Russia.
1929	A worldwide economic depression begins.
1939	World War II begins.
1945	World War II ends.
1969	Humans land on the Moon.
1975	The Vietnam War ends.
1989	The Berlin Wall is torn down as communism crumbles in Eastern Europe.
1991	The Soviet Union breaks into separate states.
2001	Terrorists attack the World Trade Center in New York City and the Pentagon near Washington, D.C.
2004	A tsunami in the Indian Ocean destroys coastlines in Africa, India, and Southeast Asia.
2008	The United States elects its first African American president.
2016	Donald Trump is elected U.S. president.

Fast Facts

Official name: People's Republic of China

Capital: Beijing

Official language: Putonghua (Standard Mandarin)

Beijing

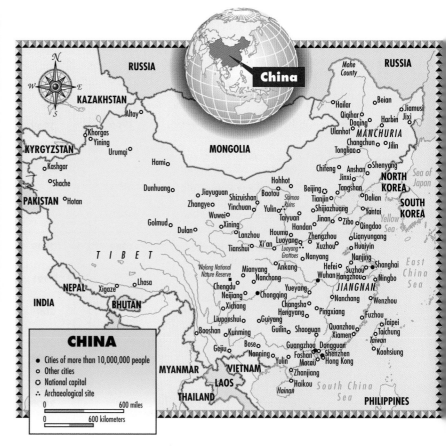

National flag

Himalayas

Official religion:	None
National anthem:	"March of the Volunteers"
Government:	Single-party communist state
Head of state:	President
Head of government:	Premier
Area of country:	3,692,260 square miles (9,562,910 sq km)
Latitude and longitude of geographic center:	103.23° E, 35.33° N
Bordering countries:	Russia and Mongolia to the north; North Korea to the east; Vietnam, Laos, Myanmar, India, Bhutan, and Nepal to the south; Pakistan, Afghanistan, Tajikistan, Kyrgyzstan, and Kazakhstan to the west
Highest elevation:	Mount Everest, 29,035 feet (8,850 m) above sea level
Lowest elevation:	Ayding Lake within the Turpan Depression, 505 feet (154 m) below sea level
Highest average temperature:	Fuzhou, with average July highs of about 92°F (33°C)
Lowest average temperature:	Mohe County, with average January lows of −21.6°F (−29.8°C)

Shanghai

National population
(2016 est.): 1,373,541,278

Population of major
cities (2015 est.):

Shanghai	23,000,000
Beijing	18,079,000
Guangzhou	12,385,000
Shenzhen	12,337,000
Chongqing	11,054,000

Landmarks:
- ▶ *Forbidden City*, Beijing
- ▶ *Giant panda sanctuaries*, Sichuan Province
- ▶ *Great Wall*, northern China
- ▶ *Luoyang Grottoes*, Luoyang
- ▶ *Terra-cotta army*, Xi'an

Economy: China has one of the world's largest economies. It is a world leader in mining of ores such as iron, zinc, and lead. It is also the world's largest manufacturer, producing steel, aluminum, textiles, cement, chemicals, consumer products, and much more. China's leading agriculture products include rice, wheat, corn, potatoes, peanuts, chickens, pigs, and fish. It is one of the world's most popular tourist destinations.

Currency: The Chinese currency is the renminbi, and the basic unit is called the yuan. In 2017, 1 yuan equaled 15 U.S. cents, and 6.88 yuan equaled US$1.

Currency

System of weights
and measures: China uses the metric system as the standard, and many people still use part of an ancient system.

Literacy rate (2015): 96.4%

Schoolchildren

Yao Ming

Common Mandarin Chinese phrases:

Ni hao ma	How are you?
Wo xing . . .	My name is . . .
Zao an	Good morning
Wan an	Good evening
Xie xie	Thank you
Zhu ni hao yun	Good luck
Ni hao	Hello
Qing wen	Excuse me
Dui bu qi	Sorry
Ma fan ni	Please
Zao ri kang fu	Get well soon

Prominent Chinese:

Bai Juyi   (772–846 CE)
Poet and government official

Confucius   (551 BCE–479 BCE)
Philosopher

Deng Xiaoping   (1904–1997)
Communist leader and reformer

Li Na   (1982–)
Tennis player

Mao Zedong   (1893–1976)
Political and military leader

Mo Yan   (1955–)
Nobel Prize–winning writer

Qin Shi Huang   (259 BCE–210 BCE)
First emperor of China

Yao Ming   (1980–)
Basketball player

To Find Out More

Books

▶ Cohn, Jessica. *The Ancient Chinese*. New York: Gareth Stevens Publishing, 2013.

▶ Ganeri, Anita. *Chinese Myths and Legends*. Chicago: Capstone Raintree, 2013.

▶ Luh, Shu Shin. *The People of China*. Philadelphia: Mason Crest, 2013.

▶ Roxburgh, Ellis. *The Chinese Empire*. New York: Cavendish Square Publishing, 2016.

▶ Sonneborn, Liz. *Ancient China*. New York: Children's Press, 2012.

Videos

▶ *Beijing: The Capital of China*. Travel Video Store, 2014.

▶ *Discover the World: China*. Travel Video Store, 2013.

▶ *In the North and South of the Great Wall*. Travel Video Store, 2012.

▶ Visit this Scholastic website for more information on China:
www.factsfornow.scholastic.com
Enter the keyword China

Index

Page numbers in *italics* indicate illustrations.

famine, 56–57, 74
"Feelings on Watching the Moon"
	(Bai Juyi), 109
Festivals of the Living, 124–127
fishing industry, 80, *81*, 89
Five Dynasties and Ten Kingdoms
	period, 49
flooding, 22, *22*, 23
folk music, 112
foods, 32, 74, *75*, 86, 117, 118, *118*,
	119–121, *119*, *120*, 121–122, *121*,
	123, 126–127
Forbidden City, 71, *71*
fossils, 39
Foxy Lady (musical group), 112
Fu Han, 112
Fujian Province, 77, 112
funerals, 69, 107
Fuzhou, 18

G
games, 122, 125, 126
Genghis Khan, 51
geography
	borders, 15, 19
	Central Uplands, 20
	coastline, 15, 20
	deserts, 17, *17*
	diversity of, 9
	earthquakes, 20, *20*
	Eastern Highlands, 19
	Eastern Lowlands, 19
	elevation, 16, 18, 27
	islands, 15, 20
	karst hills, *14*
	lakes, 18, 24–25, *24*
	land area, 15
	loess, 17, 23, *23*
	mountains, 16, *16*, 17, 18, 19, *19*,
		20, 27
	plateaus, 16, 17, 20
	rivers, 16, 19, *19*, 20, 21–24, *21*,
		22, 27

	Sichuan Basin, 20
	Southern Uplands, 20
	uplands, 17
Germany, 52
giant pandas, 36, *36*
ginkgo trees, 33, *33*
ginseng, 31
Gobi Desert, 17, *17*
government. *See also* dynasties.
	administrative divisions, 67–68, *67*
	agriculture and, 56, 74, 75, 85
	appointments to, 62
	autonomous regions, 68
	censorship, 103
	Chinese Communist Party (CCP),
		54–55, *55*, 56–57, 60, 61, 62,
		65, 70, 103, 123, 133
	communism, 12
	Confucianism and, 98
	constitution, 65, 95
	Cultural Revolution, 57, *57*
	democracy and, 61–62
	Deng Xiaoping, 58, 75, 133
	economy and, 55, 56, 58, 73, 85
	education and, 93
	elections, 61–62, *62*, 63
	executive branch, 62–64, *64*
	foreign policy, 70
	Han dynasty, 46
	housing and, 123
	judicial branch, 63, 66–67
	language and, 93
	legislative branch, 54, 63, 66
	Local People's Courts, 66–67
	Mao Zedong, 12–13, *12*, 54, 55,
		56, *56*, 57, *57*, 70, 74, 133
	military, 69, 70
	municipalities, 68
	Nationalist Party, 54, 55, *55*
	National People's Congress
		(NPC), 63, 65–66, *65*

	one-child policy, 86
	pollution and, 25
	population and, 86
	presidents, 54, 58, 63, 64, *64*, 103
	protests, 58–59, *59*
	regional government, 67–68, *68*
	religion and, 95, 96
	special administrative regions
		(SARs), 68
	Standing Committee, 66
	State Administration for Religious
		Affairs (SARA), 97
	State Council, 64
	Supreme People's Court, 66, *66*
	urban relocation and, 85, 90
	welfare policy, 50
	writing system and, 93
Grand Canal, *47*
Great Britain, 52
Great Hall of the People, 74
Great Wall of China, 43, 44, *44*, 51
gross domestic product (GDP), 78
Guangdong Province, 77
Guangxi Autonomous Region, 88
Guangzhou. *See also* cities.
	Baomo Garden, 29
	Bright Filial Piety Temple, 29
	as capital city, 29
	founding of, 29, *52*
	population, 29, 86
	Yuexiu Park, 29
Guizhou Province, *13*
guqin (musical instrument), 111, *112*

H
Haikou, 27
Hainan Island, 20, 27, 87
Hainan Province, *81*
Hall of Prayer for Good Harvests, *94*
Han dynasty, 45–46, 87
Hanggai (musical group), 112
Han people, 87, *87*, 88, 89

Ox Street Mosque, 71
Silk Road and, 100
State Administration for Religious
  Affairs (SARA), 97
Temple of Heaven, *94*
renminbi (currency), 74
reptilian life, 34
Republic of China, 54, 56
rice, 20, 39, 44, 120, 122
roadways, 25, 43, 82
Russia, 52
Ru Zhijuan, 108

S

saxaul shrub, 33
sculpture, 105–106, *105*, *106*
service industries, 80–81
Qinghai Province, *22*
Shaanxi Province
  archaeology in, 41, *41*
  earthquake in, 20
  Long March, 55
  terra-cotta army, 45, *45*
  Terracotta Army Museum, 45
Shandong Peninsula, 19
Shandong Province, 52, 74, 98
Shang dynasty, 40–41
Shanghai. *See also* cities.
  architecture, 29, *29*
  automobiles in, 83
  government and, 68
  Great Britain and, 52
  location of, 19
  manufacturing in, 29
  Oriental Pearl Tower, 29, *29*
  population of, 29, 86
  roadways in, *8*
  Shanghai World Financial Center,
    29
Shan Hai Jing (Mountain and Sea
  Scroll), 101
Shen Kuo, 108
Shenzhen, 29, 83, 86

Shimao Ruins, 41, *41*
Shuanglong Lake, *24*
Sichuan Basin, 20
Sichuan Province, 36
silk, *10*, 39, *47*, 52, 106, 112
Silk Road, 46, *46*, 48, 100
snub-nosed monkeys, 35, *35*
Song dynasty, 49–51, *49*, 100
The Song of Everlasting Sorrow (Wang
  Anyi), 108
Song of Eternal Sorrow (Bai Juyi), 109
South China Sea, 24
Southern Uplands, 20
special administrative regions (SARs),
  68, *68*
Special Economic Zones (SEZs), 73,
  77
sports, 64, 113–115, *113*, *115*, 133,
  133
Spring Festival, 124–125
Standing Committee, 66
State Administration for Religious
  Affairs (SARA), 97
State Council, 64
steamed foods, 121
steel industry, 78, *78*
stir-frying, 121, *121*
Sui dynasty, 47, *47*
Sun Tian Tian, 114
Sun Yat-sen, 54, *54*
Supreme People's Court, 66, *66*

T

table tennis, 114–115, *115*
Taiwan, 15, 56, 93
Taklimakan Desert, 17
Tang dynasty, 48, *48*, 108, 109, 110
Tangshan, 20
technology industries, 29
Temple of Confucius, 98
Temple of Heaven, *94*, 71
tennis, 114
Terracotta Army Museum, 45
theater, 110–111, *110*
Three Principles of the People, 54

Tiananmen Square, 59, 70, 71, 98,
  105
Tian Han, 69
Tianjin, *53*, 68, 83
Tibetan language, 90
Tibetan people, 88, 90, *90*
Tibetan Plain, 87
Tibet Autonomous Region, 35
timber industry, 19
tones, 91–93
tourism, 25, 36, 71, 80–81
trade, 46, *46*, 48, 51, 52, *52*
transportation, 24, 25, 81–83, *83*
Tujia people, 88
Turpan Depression, 17, *18*
typhoons, 28, *28*

U

United States
  Boxer Rebellion and, *53*
  foreign affairs and, 70
  music in, 112
  National Basketball Association
    (NBA), 113, 114
  Olympic Games and, 115
  tourism and, 81
Uyghur people, 88, 89, *89*

V

villages. *See also* cities.
  early settlers, 39
  elections in, 62
  Shenzhen as, 29
  Tibetans and, 90
  urban relocation, 85, 90

W

Wang Anyi, 108
Wang Shimin, *104*
Wang Wei, 109
Wei dynasty, 100
weights and measurements, 76, *76*

wildlife. *See* amphibian life; animal
    life; insect life; marine life; plant
    life; reptilian life.
Wolong National Nature Reserve, 36
Women's Chinese Basketball
    Association, 113
woodblock printing, 48, 108
World War II, 55
writing system, 93
Wuhan, *22*

X

Xia dynasty, 40
Xi'an, 45
Xi Jinping, 58, 64, 103
Xinjiang Autonomous Region, 80, 82,
    89, 89
Xinjiang-Mongolian Uplands, 17
Xinjiang region, 35
Xi River, 20, 21, 24

Y

yaks, *34*, 35
Yangtze River, 16, 18, 19, 21–22, *21*,
    22, 24, 27, 29, 36, 87
Yao Ming, 113, 114, *114*, 133, *133*
Yellow River, 16, 19, 21, 22–23, 27,
    87
Yellow Sea, 22
Ying Zheng, 42–43, *43*
Yi people, 88
yuan (currency), 74, *74*
Yuan dynasty, 51, 71
Yuexiu Park, 29

Z

Zeng Liansong, 70
Zhou dynasty, 41–42, 106
Zhou Qunfei, 82
Zhuang people, 88, *88*

Meet the Author

NEL YOMTOV IS AN AWARD-WINNING author who has written nonfiction books and graphic novels about American and world history, geography, science, mythology, sports, and careers. He has written numerous books in Scholastic's Enchantment of the World series, including *Scotland*, *Syria*, *Costa Rica*, *Israel*, *Russia*, and others.

Yomtov was born in New York City. He worked at Marvel Comics as a writer, editor, colorist, and director of product development. He has served as editorial director of a large children's book publisher and as publisher of the Hammond World Atlas book division. In addition, Yomtov was a consultant to Major League Baseball, where he helped develop an educational program for elementary and middle schools throughout the country.

Yomtov lives in the New York area with his wife, Nancy, a teacher. His son, Jess, is a sports journalist.

Photo Credits

Photographs ©: